BENT'S OLD FORT

3 1717 00037 7186

Library of Congress Catalog Card No. 78-740 21

Printed by Williams Printing
4805 Northpark Drive
Colorado Springs
Colorado 80907

343

Seven miles east of La Junta on Colorado Highway 194, Bent's Old Fort National Historic Site was officially dedicated at ceremonies on 25 July 1976. Colorado Governor Richard Lamm, Department of the Interior officials, National Park Service staff, and several thousand visitors marveled at the re-created adobe castle rising majestically on the Colorado high plains. Their trip into the past was enhanced by costumed interpreters cast in the roles of the trading post's occupants of 130 years ago. Additional thousands of sightseers have since wandered through the authentically reproduced fort, the replica of a once self-sufficient outpost and the center of a Southwestern trading empire. Bent's Old Fort is a monument to the Bicentennial of our nation and to the Colorado Centennial.

A modern-day, mountain man color guard initiates the Sunday afternoon dedication ceremonies, an occasion for stirring, patriotic music.

*Native cere-
monial dances
remind on-
lookers that
Bent's Old
Fort was a
center for trade
for many
southwestern
tribes. Col-
orado Gover-
nor Richard D.
Lamm
addresses ded-
ication cere-
mony visitors
on the signifi-
cance of the
National Park
Service recon-
struction.*

Under the hot July sun, the visitors gathered
to enjoy the colorful dances in the plaza and
the chants to the sound of the drums,
chants done in the tradition of the ancestors
who once camped beside the adobe walls of the fort.
And, Colorado Governor Lamm hobnobs with some contemporary
mountain men outside of the walls of the fort.

Life in an Adobe Castle, 1833-1849

BY ENID THOMPSON

Bent's Old Fort was an outpost of American civilization situated on the southwestern edge of the American frontier. A symbol of Manifest Destiny, the fort was located on the Mountain Branch of the Santa Fe Trail, the crossroads of trade among the Indians of the plains, the trappers of the mountains, and the traders of the Southwest. Bent's Old Fort was the largest of all the trading posts in the mountain-plains region. The people who built and maintained the fort, and many of those who visited it,

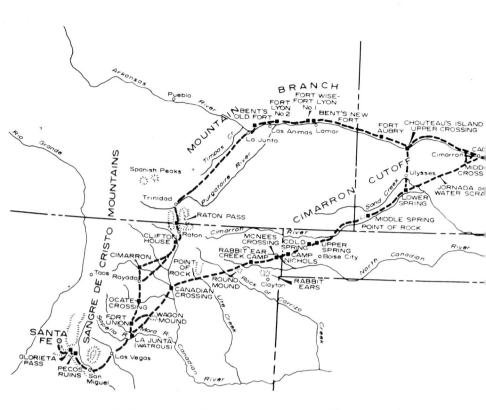

were, in large part, the people who, guided by economic necessity and commercial acumen, carried forward the Americanization of the area during the 1830s and 1840s.

In the 1830s the trade on the Santa Fe Trail was increasing as the fur trade market was decreasing. With the beaver virtually trapped out of the Missouri River drainage area and the introduction of the silk hat into European and American fashion, the fur trade market was severely affected. The independent trappers, such as Ceran St. Vrain and William and Charles Bent, were then forced south into the Arkansas River valley in pursuit of the beaver, where they were exposed to the embryonic but highly lucrative Santa Fe trade. The Cheyenne had crossed the South Platte River and entered the upper Arkansas River region by 1827, opening up a whole new trading area.

In addition to changing trade patterns, Mexican gold and silver were desperately needed on the specie-short American frontier during this era. In November 1831 the *Saint Louis Beacon* called the supply of Mexican gold and silver a guarantee to the continued commercial preeminence and prosperity of Saint Louis. Thus, from small beginnings in the 1820s, the trade from Santa Fe to Saint Louis had grown into a million-dollar-a-year business by the 1840s.

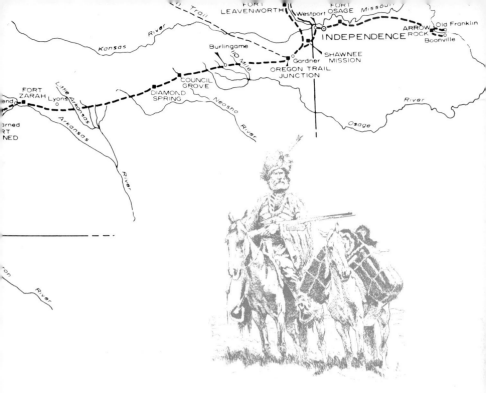

Hoping to cash in on this trade, in December 1830 while William Bent was trapping in the New Mexican mountains, Ceran St. Vrain and Charles Bent formed a partnership so that one of them could tend to the trade in Taos while the other could freight their trade goods on the Santa Fe Trail. By 1832 news of the partnership of the Bents and St. Vrain had spread eastward. On 10 January 1834 William Laidlaw, an American Fur Company trader at Fort Pierre in present-day South Dakota, wrote to Pierre Chouteau in Saint Louis that "I understand from the Sioux that Charles Bent has built a Fort upon the Arkansas for the purpose of trade with the different bands of Indians."[1] While the name of the partnership seems to have varied over the first few years, by 1833 it had become known as Bent, St. Vrain & Company. The partnership continued until 1848, when St. Vrain left and went into business in Santa Fe, and William, as the sole surviving Bent, continued the business at Bent's Old Fort until 1849.

Sources for this article, except for the direct quotations, will not be cited in footnotes. The "Bibliographical Note" dealing with Bent's Old Fort and the various aspects of the southwestern frontier suggests the sources for this historical overview of the early history of the fort.

[1] William Laidlaw, Fort Pierre, to Pierre Chouteau, Esq., 10 January 1834, Upper Missouri Outfit, Letter Book B, Chouteau Papers, Missouri Historical Society, St. Louis. The letter is cited in LeRoy R. Hafen, "When Was Bent's Fort Built?" *The Colorado Magazine* 31 (April 1954):117.

Charles Bent   *William Bent*

Charles and William Bent were ideally suited to their unique business. They were the grandsons of Silas Bent, who had led the "Indians" during the American Revolution in throwing the taxed tea into Boston harbor. Their father, Silas Bent, Jr., was a prominent judge who in 1806 was appointed surveyor-general of the Louisiana Territory, with headquarters in Saint Louis. As youths, the brothers had worked in Saint Louis for the veteran fur trade firm of Manuel Lisa and Joshua Pilcher.

The home of Silas Bent, Jr., and the Bent family on the bank of the Mississippi River near Saint Louis.

Both of the Bent brothers were small in stature, Charles topping William at a height of five feet seven inches. With swarthy complexions, at times they were mistaken for French-Canadians, and both maintained open relations with the Indians. Cheyenne Chief Yellow Wolf, leader of the Hairy Rope band, gave Charles the name White Hat and William, Little White Man. While Charles did most of the freighting and buying, skillfully managing affairs in Saint Louis and in Santa Fe, William's chief contribution to the trading company was his knowledge of and ability to deal with the Plains Indians. Indeed, about 1836 William married Owl Woman, the daughter of a Cheyenne chief, thus cementing his relations with that tribe. And it was William who supervised the construction and the maintenance of Bent's Old Fort.

Their partner Ceran St. Vrain was born in Missouri, the son of a noble family dispossessed during the French Revolution of 1789. His uncle, Charles Auguste de Lassus, had been lieutenant-governor of Louisiana under both French and Spanish rule. St. Vrain had good connections in Saint Louis, where he was regarded as a polished, urbane, and gracious Frenchman. He was also respected in Santa Fe, where he became a naturalized Mexican citizen, spoke Spanish elegantly, and shared the Catholic religion of the New Mexicans. His connections in New Mexico were invaluable to the Bents, and his knowledge of New Mexican architecture and workmanship may well have been the dominant reason for the structural uniqueness of the adobe fort that was built on the Arkansas River.

The Bents and St. Vrain, supposedly with the help of Cheyenne Chief Yellow Wolf, selected the north bank, or the American side of the Arkansas River, thirty miles above Big Timbers, for the site to build their trading fort. The location took into consideration the traffic on the Trappers Trail between Santa Fe and Fort Laramie, the Taos trade commerce, between Santa Fe and Saint Louis, and the potential for barter with the Mountain Ute, the Kiowa, the Arapaho, the Pawnee, and the Cheyenne.

While the fort was known to its builders as Fort William, for William Bent, history has designated the post as Bent's Fort. It is more often called Bent's Old Fort, to distinguish it from the stone fort that William built down river on the Arkansas in 1853. The date of the actual building of Bent's Old Fort is still a subject of discussion. Historians of the fort, David Lavender, LeRoy R. Hafen, and George Hammond, are in agreement that

An 1843 note signed at Bent's Old Fort (Fort William) on the Arkansas River indebted trapper William S. Williams to Bent, St. Vrain & Company for the use of four "Beaver Traps" and for $300 payable in "good merchantable Beaver."

1833 is the year of construction. However, Charles W. Hurd places the date as early as 1828 or 1829. The first official notice of the fort was the Laidlaw letter dated 10 January 1834. Thus, 1833 is probably the correct year marking the completion of the imposing castle on the banks of the Arkansas River.

According to historical records, the fort was essentially an adobe built compound, measuring 142 feet by 122 feet. It was composed of twenty-six one- or two-story apartments that surrounded a graveled placita. Two corrals, one on the east, and a larger one on the southwest, with attendant wagon sheds and walls, provided protection for the wagons and stock. Inside the walls were a well, storerooms, mechanics' areas, living quarters, and recreational facilities. Outside the gates of the fort were an ice house, a trash dump, a racetrack, and a burial ground. Round bastions towered at the northeast and southwest corners of the structure, and a watchtower, with flag flying, provided a guard post above the main gate. The four rows of rooms around the placita were assigned various functions. The public rooms — the council room, the store, and the dining room — were on the south. The smithy, carpenter shop, and offices were on the west. Storerooms were located on the north, and the living quarters and trade rooms were stationed on the east.

One early visitor to the fort surmised that it was "capable of accommodating 100 men," and he noted that within its walls were "1000 stand of arms and 1 brass cannon." A Saint Louis newspaper reported in 1846 that the fort was "constructed of what is termed in New Mexico adobes — a sun dried brick, which becomes hard and firm and durable. They are 18 inches long, 9 inches wide, and 4 inches thick. They are not made with as much precision as our brick but when put up, make a wall that is strong and passable."[2]

An 1839 sojourner was also much impressed by the defensive capacities of the fortification. "Fort William would prove impregnable, for the red devils would never dream of scaling the walls," commented New Orleans newspaperman Matthew C. Field. The journalist noted that the structure could garrison 200 men in his exciting description of a Comanche raid on Bent's Old Fort. Seventy-five valuable animals were driven away by

    [2] Obadiah Oakley, "Oregon Expedition (1839)," *Peoria* (Ill.) *Register*, [?] 1914, clipping file, New York City Public Library; *Saint Louis Weekly Reveille*, 18 May 1846, *Reveille* file, Missouri Historical Society, St. Louis. *See also* Nolie Mumey, *Old Forts and Trading Posts of the West* (Denver: Artcraft Press, 1956)1: 25, 35.

twenty Comanches on swift mounts, and "the hapless Spaniard who had been on duty [outside of the gates] was seen to stagger toward the fort, and fall with three barbed arrows quivering in his body."[3]

Significant as it was along lines of military capability, the occupants of Bent's Old Fort were more concerned with establishing trade with the Indians than they were with fighting them. Perhaps the most important visitor in terms of offering an accurate picture of the fort, Lieutenant James W. Abert of the

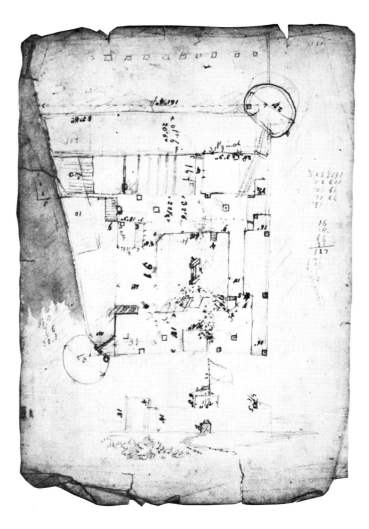

United States Topographical Engineers, stayed at the adobe outpost twice, once in 1845 and again in 1846, when he was recuperating from an illness. Describing the peace talks of 1845, Abert noted how the Indians and the whites negotiated frontier style, seated on buffalo robes scattered over the council chamber's dirt floor. At the time of his 1846 visit, while convalescing during his second stay, Abert measured and sketched the fort, providing the most complete extant drawings of the structure. The lieutenant made mention of one of the employees at the fort, John Simpson Smith, commenting on his remarkable facility with Indian languages.[4]

A workable relationship with the Indians, then, was a central factor affecting trade. And work was the foundation of the social structure at Bent's Old Fort. During the early and the mid-nineteenth century, a high degree of social prestige was attached to the position of entrepreneur, but that prestige did not ensure leisure. The Bents and St. Vrain were hard workers, often away from the fort on freighting trips or on trading expeditions. For their principal assistants they relied heavily on family members. George and Robert Bent and Marcellin St. Vrain, all younger brothers, were included in the business. The family group encompassed relatives by marriage as well. The training of these principal assistants was conducted under the apprenticeship method, by which Charles and William Bent had been trained in Saint Louis.

Important as relatives were in keeping the business functioning, independent trappers were always welcome at the fort. Usually they were accorded the respect due free agents and entrepreneurs. On the other hand, hired trappers, traders, hunters, and guides were considered less impressive socially, until, as in the case of Kit Carson, they achieved a measure of success on their own. Yet even though Carson was a respected member of the company, legend has it that he was not allowed to marry Felicite St. Vrain, the boss's niece. Carson, the father of a half-breed daughter, was apparently an unacceptable suitor. Evidently the fort's cultural pluralism, with all its elastic standards, was not quite broad enough to encompass such a marriage.

[3] Matthew Field, "Fort William," *New Orleans Picayune,* 12 July 1840; *see also* Thomas J. Farnham, *Travels in the Great Western Prairies, the Anahuac and Rocky Mountains,* . . . (London: Richard Bentley, 1843), reprinted in *Early Western Travels . . . during the Period of Early American Settlement,* ed. Reuben G. Thwaites (Cleveland, Ohio: Arthur H. Clark Co., 1906), 28: 164-65.

[4] Lieutenant James W. Abert, *Journal of Lieutenant J. W. Abert from Bent's Fort to St. Louis, in 1845,* U.S., Congress, Senate, *Senate Document No. 438,* 29th Cong., 1st sess., 1846, p. 5.

The fort was a focal point for diverse cultural interaction. At least seven languages — English, French, Spanish, Sioux, Cheyenne, Ute, and Comanche — were spoken there. Color, race, and religion usually seemed to have carried only a little weight as to social credentials; Bent's slave cook, Charlotte Green, and the Black mountain man Jim Beckwourth were respected workers and individuals. Mexicans, however, who filled the more menial jobs, lacked social standing at the fort. Indians, excepting the wives and children of inhabitants, were not allowed in the fort overnight.

Possibly, this hierarchy is best illustrated by the seating arrangements in the fort's dining room. From eight to twenty persons took dinner there, entertained by the highest ranking official in the firm, who served as the host. Historian Francis Parkman noted the same ranking at Fort Laramie:

> The discordant jingling of a bell . . . summoned us to supper. This sumptuous repast was served on a rough table in one of the lower apartments of the fort, and consisted of cakes of bread and dried buffalo meat — an excellent thing for strengthening the teeth. At this meal were seated the *bourgeois* and superior dignitaries of the establishment. . . . No sooner was it finished, than the table was spread a second time (the luxury of bread now being, however, omitted), for the benefit of certain hunters and trappers of an inferior standing; while the ordinary . . . *engages* were regaled on dried meat in one of their lodging rooms.[5]

At Bent's Old Fort, too, the temporary help was not admitted to the dining room. Freighters and other transients were not even assigned sleeping rooms. They stored their goods and equipment in the wagon house and cooked and ate in an eight-man mess just as they did on the trail. Most of their recreation was found with others in their own group. Except for the security afforded by the walls, they might just as well have been camped on the plains.

The full-time staff of the fort, the artisans and mechanics, were provided with living quarters, and usually they had their wives and children to live with them. This group included a carpenter, a blacksmith, a gunsmith, a wheelwright, a cook, a tailor, and sometimes a barber. This nucleus of employees comprised the stable population of the fort, supervised by the factor

---

[5] Francis Parkman, *The Oregon Trail: Sketches of Prairie and Rocky-Mountain Life*, ed. Charles H. J. Douglas (New York: Macmillan Co., 1914), p. 93.

George Bent, a younger brother, and his Cheyenne wife Magpie, the niece of Chief Black Kettle, sat for their portrait in 1867.

or clerk. They were supplemented by a floating population of herders, bullwhackers, women who came to repair adobe, horse wranglers and breakers, makers of hay, hunters, and others.

This host of people was assembled for the primary purpose of trade. Initially Saint Louis purchases contracted by the Bents and St. Vrain were for Indian trade goods. Such items included axes, blankets, knives, powder horns, guns, kettles, an assortment of beads, and other goods in demand among the Indian tribes. (The medium of exchange at the fort was usually cured buffalo hides or peltries.) A different category of merchandise was purchased for the Santa Fe trade. This extension in the fort's commercial linkage secured Mexican gold and silver instead of hides. Materials for trade in Santa Fe included a variety of cloth and clothing, sugar, coffee, rice, tea, cutlery, domestic items, and barrels of rum and stills. Bent's Old Fort stood as a major transfer point in an intricate and often lucrative system of interchange.

The trade empire of Bent, St. Vrain & Company (about 1840, bounded by heavy line) extended into nine present-day western states. The Taos Trail (. . . .) carried the Bent, St. Vrain trade into New Mexico, where Charles Bent and later Ceran St. Vrain established residence in Taos.

The full complement of permanent residents at the fort who kept the goods moving was about twenty, but on occasion only eight to twelve persons would be present. With the return of everyone who had been working in the field, the camps, or on the trail, the population of the fort could swell to between one hundred fifty and two hundred persons. The organization and discipline necessary to maintain an operation on the scale of

Bent's Old Fort required exceptional management skills, particularly considering the free-wheeling nature of many of the characters who comprised the company.

Indeed, a list of persons who visited or worked at Bent's Old Fort would read like a "Who's Who of the West." Kit Carson, for example, gave up trapping to become a hunter at the fort in 1840. Alexander Barclay, a self-proclaimed partner in the fort, was hired as a clerk by George Bent in Saint Louis in 1838. Barclay served as factor during the remodeling of the fort in 1840, when its defenses were expanded and improved. Two years later he left Bent's employ to trade first at Pueblo, then Hardscrabble, and ultimately to build Barclay's Fort at Moro, New Mexico. Another fort builder, Lancaster Lupton, initially saw the fort in 1835 while serving as a lieutenant in the First Dragoons under Colonel Henry Dodge.[6] Later, he was the builder and the owner of Fort Lupton on the South Platte River in Colorado.

The free traders and trappers who frequented the fort were among the best known of the mountain men, including James Baker, Thomas Fitzpatrick, Francis Robidoux, and "Uncle Dick" Wootton. Among the better known of the fort's visitors, who were also the chroniclers of the fort, were Lewis Garrard, Francis Parkman, Thomas Farnham, William Boggs, Albert G. Boone, Susan Magoffin, and of course, the convalescing Lieutenant Abert.

In addition to the passing parade of military visitors, a school teacher and a medical doctor once resided at the fort. George Simpson, after whom Simpson's Rest near present-day Trinidad was named, was a school teacher at the fort, dressed in a frock coat and a silk hat. The physician was Dr. Edward L. Hempstead, a member of a prominent Saint Louis family and a nephew of Manuel Lisa by marriage. Hempstead lived at the adobe outpost for several years. The "resident physician's" presence was noted by Garrard, who provided some entertaining descriptions of social conditions at the fort in 1847. Along with his notations on the famed billiard room and the "first-rate spy-glass" in the clerk's office, Garrard observed that the fort's "mud walls were abominably cheerless."

As Garrard soon learned, residents at the fort had to make

---

[6] Colonel Henry Dodge, *Journal of the March of a Detachment of U.S. Dragoons, under Command of Colonel Dodge, into the Indian Country during the Summer of 1835, American State Papers: Military Affairs*, vol. 6, 1835; U.S. Congress, House, *House Document No. 181*, 24th Cong., 1st sess., 1836, pp. 23-25.

their own cheer. And they appear to have been quite capable of combating the loneliness attendant to life on an isolated frontier. One source of amusement was created in nightly dances. The carpenter's wife Rosalie, a "half-breed French and Indian squaw," and Charlotte, "the culinary divinity," — a duo described by a Missouri teamster as the "only female women" at the fort — were "swung rudely and gently in the mazes of the contra dance" every evening. "Such a medley of steps is seldom seen out of the mountains," said Garrard, "— the halting, irregular march of the war dance, the slipping gallopade, the boisterous pitching of the Missouri backwoodsman, and the more nice gyrations of the Frenchmen — for all, irrespective of rank, age, and *color*, went pellmell into the excitement."[7] During these particular festivities, at least, any social formalities at the fort broke down under the hilarity of the moment.

Rosalie and Charlotte may have been the "belles of the evening" at these delightful interludes, but they were not the only women at the fort. Hunters, trappers, and traders alike often took Indians for wives. William Bent had married the Cheyenne Owl Woman, and after she died while giving birth to their fourth child, he married one of her sisters, Yellow Woman. Marcellin St. Vrain, Ceran's younger brother, had a Sioux girl for his first wife. During his residence at Bent's Old Fort between 1845 and 1848 he took a second Indian wife known as Big Pawnee Woman, whom he left behind when he returned to Saint Louis in 1848. Desertion of Indian wives and half-breed children was not unusual, since it was acceptable according to Indian custom.

Interracial marriage at the fort offers another perspective from which to examine frontier pluralism. Susan Shelby Magoffin, who celebrated her nineteenth birthday at the adobe "castle" on 30 July 1846, confided to her diary concerning the Mexican women visiting the fort. Several days before she gave birth to a stillborn child, the young wife was well enough to socialize as she waited for her quarters to be prepared. In a large room that she described as the "parlor," which had no chairs but was equipped with a cushion next to the wall, the company sat in a circle. The only furniture was a table, which held a "bucket of water, free to all." In these surroundings the pregnant frontierswoman visited with "*las senoritas*, the wife of Mr. George

⁷ Lewis A. Garrard, *Wah-To-Yah and the Taos Trail, Southwest Historical Series*, ed. Ralph P. Bieber (Glendale, Calif.: Arthur H. Clark Co., 1938), 6:129.

Susan Shelby Magoffin

Bent and some others. One of them sat and combed her hair while notwithstanding the presence of Mr. Lighten[s]doffer whose lady (a Mexican) was present. After the combing she paid her devoirs to a crock of oil or greese [*sic*] of some kind, and it is not exaggeration to say it almost *driped* [*sic*] from her hair to the floor. If I had not seen her at it, I never would have believed it greese [*sic*], but that she had been washing her head."[8]

Magoffin and the other visitors are important, not only because they left the only written descriptions of conditions and life at the adobe compound, but also because they ably demonstrate another significant function of Bent's Old Fort. A symbol of Manifest Destiny due to its very existence on the

[8] Susan Shelby Magoffin, *Down the Santa Fe Trail and into Mexico: The Diary of Susan Shelby Magoffin, 1846-47,* ed. Stella M. Drumm (New Haven, Conn.: Yale University Press, 1926), pp. 61-63.

outskirts of the frontier, a gathering place for sundry cultures, and most importantly a complex institution organized for trade, the fort was also a way station or "hotel" for travelers on the Santa Fe Trail. It provided security, company, and a quality of accommodation otherwise lacking between Saint Louis and Santa Fe.

Both food and lodging varied within the fort. Private quarters of considerable luxury were available for the proprietors and the principal employees. On occasion these rooms were loaned to guests. The married quarters, where families lived and cooked together, were fashioned on a barracks plan similar to the New Mexican hacienda. The fort's dormitories housed six to eight men in comfort but austerity. A number of private rooms, Spartan but clean, were available for travelers. Finally, there was the council room, where Mexican style beds could be spread out for transients. Unfortunately, no records exist to show if the guests at Bent's Old Fort were charged for their accommodations. It is quite probable, however, that upper echelon travelers received their lodgings gratis as the guests of the proprietors.

In accord with its hotel function, the fort sometimes provided the services of a hospital as well. Ordinarily, when Dr. Hempstead was not on the premises, William Bent served as the resident physician, not infrequently calling upon Indian medicine men for aid. Rendering medical assistance became particularly valuable during the Mexican War between 1846 and 1848. Colonel Alexander W. Doniphan left twenty-one sick Missouri Volunteers at the adobe outpost, and sixty of General Stephen W. Kearny's soldiers, one of whom was Lieutenant Abert, found a place to recuperate behind the walls of the fort.

Employment of the fort as a military medical facility sheds light on another of its functions, that of an unofficial United States Army outpost. Susan Magoffin commented on the presence of the Army of the West in the summer of 1846. "There is the greatest possible noise in the patio," she wrote in her diary. "The shoeing of horses, neighing, and braying of mules, the crying of children, the scolding and fighting of men, are all enough to turn my head . . . . The Fort is crowded to overflowing." When General Kearny's troops were on hand, "the clang of the blacksmith's hammer was constant. The trumpet sounded oft and loud; swords rattled in their sheths [sic], while the tinkling spur served as an echo. Ever and anon some military command was heard issuing, and doubtless promptly answered."[9]

At the outbreak of the Mexican War, Stephen Watts Kearny (1794-1848) was made commander of the Army of the West with the rank of brigadier general.

It was at Bent's Old Fort that the Army of the West came together in its entirety. Only the highest in command received quarters within the fort itself. Following their arrival on 28 July, the balance of the army was stationed at various points around the fort's walls. By 2 August a majority of the soldiers had left to do battle with the Mexicans. Even though the clamor of troops had passed, the fort retained certain obligations to the army. Aside from its hospital uses, the fort served as a government supply depot into late 1847, when the army quartermaster finally departed.

Military freight and personnel overwhelmed the fort between July and October of 1846. Approximately fifty government supply wagons arrived at the outpost during a fourteen-

---

[9] Ibid., pp. 66, 67, 69.

day period in August alone. Supplies were desperately needed in recently captured Santa Fe, but military teamsters refused to take the trail beyond the fort, and so soldiers were sent to assist in forwarding the supplies. By the latter part of October, wagons were leaving the adobe castle at the rate of thirty-per-week. Bent's Old Fort, then, was an important point in an east-west transportation network in addition to its primary purpose as a trading center.

William Bent himself served in a military capacity during the Mexican conflict. He and six of his men were enlisted as a reconnaissance group to precede the army into New Mexico. Indeed, William was able to keep the Indians of the southern plains neutral during the march of the Army of the West. The nearly bloodless conquest of New Mexico was closely related to the presence of the fort on the Arkansas River and the activities of its proprietors. On 18 August 1846 General Kearny entered Santa Fe unresisted.

Prominent Mexicans had long been aware of the danger to northern Mexico created by the very presence of Bent's Old Fort. As early as the 1830s Charles Bent was actively protesting the policies of New Mexican governors. In 1840 Governor Manuel Armijo informed the Mexican government that the fort was a source of subversion. This was followed in 1845 with a warning from Santa Fe concerning the fort and Charles Bent's activities. These admonitions were justified. Charles Bent was in close touch with American authorities interested in the possibility of westward expansion. The history of these relationships can be traced in the confidential letters of the secretary of war over a number of years during the 1840s.

It is hardly surprising, then, that on 22 September 1846 Charles Bent was appointed the first American governor of New Mexico. His tenure in this capacity lasted only four months, however, for he was killed in the New Mexican uprising in Taos on 19 January 1847. General Kearny, who had made the appointment, later learned from the secretary of war that he had no legal basis for making Bent the New Mexican governor, and that, in fact, martial law would have sufficed in governing the province. Even so, while this particular appointment brought tragedy to the Bent family, it was the only payment that the Bents ever received for their many services in the cause of the Americanization of the Southwest.

William Bent was in many ways as unfortunate as Charles. His Indian trade was completely disrupted by the presence of the Army of the West in the region. He was never even paid by the army for the supplies that he provided and stored at his fort. After the death of Charles and the eventual departure of the military, William attempted as best he could to carry on his trading business, but he experienced numerous problems. In 1847, St. Vrain initiated negotiations with the army for the sale of Bent's Old Fort to the government. St. Vrain asked $15,000 for the adobe outpost that had spearheaded western advances, but the army rejected the offer. Sometime in early 1848, then, William Bent and Ceran St. Vrain settled their affairs as partners, and William became the sole owner of the fort, with St. Vrain assuming the proprietorship of the Taos and the Santa Fe stores, devoting his attention exclusively to New Mexican affairs.

Portending the boom that would follow a decade later, early in 1849 mountain men Seth Ward and William Guerrier brought Rocky Mountain gold into Bent's Old Fort on their way east with a trade caravan. But by the summer of the same year, the promise of easy wealth meant little in the face of combating disease, for cholera ravaged the frontier from Saint Louis to the Pacific Coast. Perhaps in response to the epidemic and in despair over the decline in trade, William Bent abandoned the fort, moving his goods in sixteen wagons to Big Timbers. On 21 August 1849 Leon Palladay, a Bent trader on Timpas Creek, heard a report and saw smoke rising from the burning outpost on the Arkansas River. A long debate has never been settled as to whether Bent blew up the fort and burned it, or whether he merely abandoned it and fumigated it with burning barrels of tar against the cholera.

There is no debate, however, about the importance of Bent's Old Fort to the frontier. The significance of the fort and the men who built and manned it, in the long run, was bigger than its purpose, its functions, or its personalities. The fort had a profound effect on the westward movement. In fifteen short years, the entire frontier passed through its gates: trappers, traders, merchants, an army of conquest, gold seekers, ranchers, and finally farmers. The fort was the first site of a ditch for irrigation in Colorado, and the Bents registered the first Colorado cattle brand.

Both in their business and personal affairs, the Bent brothers and St. Vrain were the instruments of history, the tools of westward expansion. Three venturesome men who sought to control a precarious commercial empire, they managed well

Ceran St. Vrain (1798-1870) terminated his interest in Bent's Old Fort in 1848 when he assumed control of the Taos and Santa Fe stores.

enough to make good names for themselves and their firm; they made reasonable amounts of money, which did not stay within the family in succeeding generations; and each played an active part in a turbulent frontier episode. As famed traveler and explorer George F. Ruxton remarked in 1847, "The solitary stranger passing this lone fort, feels proudly secure when he comes within sight of the 'stars and stripes' which float above the walls."[10] In fact, the site of Bent's Old Fort, a symbol of American civilization in the wilds, had been the focal point — the starting place and the destination—of much of the historic activity that took place in the Southwest during the 1830s and 1840s.

Formerly a librarian with the Denver Public Library and head librarian with the State Historical Society of Colorado, ENID THOMPSON holds the B.A. degree from the University of Montana and the M.A. degree from the University of Denver. A member of the Special Libraries Association, the Society of American Archivists, and the Western History Association, she researched the furnishing study for Bent's Old Fort for the National Park Service. She is currently a member of the history faculty of the University of Denver.

[10] George F. Ruxton, *Life in the Far West,* ed. LeRoy R. Hafen (Norman: University of Oklahoma Press, 1951), p. 181.

From Trading Post to
Melted Adobe, 1849-1920

BY LOUISA WARD ARPS

What happened to Bent's Old Fort on the Arkansas River between the day that William Bent loaded twenty wagons with his possessions and moved out, and the day that the La Junta Chapter of the Daughters of the American Revolution and Albert E. (A.E.) Reynolds of Denver, recognizing the importance of the fort on the historic Santa Fe Trail, dedicated a monument to mark its site? During those sixty-three years — 21 August 1849 to 5 September 1912 — the adobe walls had turned back to the earth from which they came and the marker stood alone on the flat made by a bend in the Arkansas River.

Nothing shows the isolation of Bent's Old Fort as much as the myths that immediately grew up concerning its abandonment. Who stripped it and blew up part of the walls? None of Bent's contemporaries, frontiersmen scattered up and down the Arkansas River, imagined that the prosperous and canny trader would have deliberately destroyed his feudal castle. Obviously,

Indians had done it. Some rumors even identified the culprits as Cheyenne, ignoring William Bent's firm friendship with his wife's nation.[1]

Placing the blame on the Indians began in September 1849, a month after the abandonment of the fort. James Brown, a government contractor, reported that he passed the fort to which Indians had set fire.[2] Four years later the Indians were still blamed. Solomon N. Carvalho, traveling with John Charles Frémont on the Pathfinder's fifth and last expedition to the West, wrote that "Bent's Fort . . . was recently destroyed by Indians and had not been rebuilt from the scarcity of timber in its vicinity."[3] The Indian myth grew bloodier as the years passed. In 1890 historian Hubert Howe Bancroft may have been referring to this Bent's Fort when he wrote that Indians captured the fort and slaughtered all the inmates except the owners, who were absent.[4]

By the early 1900s the stories had become less dramatic. Not only were the Indians exonerated, but so was Bent. Typical of the old-timers who held this view was A.E. Reynolds, who had come to Fort Lyon as post trader in 1867, two years before William Bent died. In 1920 he said that "Old Bent's Fort was not

Albert E. Reynolds arrived at Fort Lyon in 1867.
Photographed in March 1883 when forty-three years old, the post trader and successful mining investor would later have a vested interest in Bent's Old Fort.

destroyed by William Bent, nor by an explosion of powder. When Bent became satisfied that the government would not pay the price he asked [to sell the fort], he packed his valuables to the site of the new fort at Big Timbers, and left the old fort in charge of a few Indian dependents who did not desire to leave their homes in the Cheyenne villages near at hand."[5]

But what happened to Bent's Old Fort from 1849 to 1912, when the wind and the rain from above, the water seeping from below, and the neighbors carting off the adobe bricks, had leveled the walls? The year after Bent abandoned his trading post, the United States government officially discontinued the Bent's Fort branch of the Santa Fe Trail. From 1850 to 1861 stages carried the mail to Santa Fe over the Cimmaron Cutoff, which veered southwest from the Arkansas River a little west of Dodge City, Kansas.[6] Although the government ignored the road up the Arkansas, private parties still used it. After 1858 when Colorado gold was discovered, gold rushers traveled up the Arkansas River to Pueblo, up Fountain Creek, and to Denver via Cherry Creek. Of course, the travelers noted the ruins of Bent's Old Fort. What else was there to look at? "Nothing," wrote Lieutenant E.G. Beckwith in 1853, "can exceed the monotony of a journey along the Arkansas. Neither in the character of the country nor in any department of science, do we

[1] For persistent accounts that the fort was "blown up," *see* James H. Baker and LeRoy R. Hafen, eds. *History of Colorado,* 5 vols. (Denver: Linderman, Co., 1927), 1:318 n.83; David Lavender, *Bent's Fort* (Garden City, N.Y.: Doubleday & Co., 1954), pp. 313-16; Donald J. Berthrong, *The Southern Cheyennes* (Norman: University of Oklahoma Press, 1963), p. 114. For evidence that the fort was not "blown up," *see* Charles W. Hurd, *Bent's Stockade: Hidden in the Hills* (Las Animas, Colo.: By the Author, 1960), pp. 73-74.

William Bent only partially destroyed his fort. Presumably, he may have concentrated the powder on the west wall, where later stagecoaches entered over the debris. Only three months before, Bent had left his smaller trading post, known as Fort Adobe, on the Canadian River in Texas. Here he buried his trade goods in a hole in the floor of one room and blew up the inside walls of that room, to keep the goods from the Apache, Comanche, Kiowa, and raiding Comancheros. Perhaps this incident contributed to the story behind the explosion of Bent's Old Fort (Frederick W. Rathjen, *The Texas Panhandle Frontier* [Austin: University of Texas Press, 1973], pp. 93-94).

[2] *St. Louis Daily Missouri Republican,* 29 September 1849.

[3] Solomon N. Carvalho, *Incidents of Travel and Adventure in the Far West with Colonel Fremont's Last Expedition* . . . (New York: Derby & Jackson, 1860), p. 134.

[4] Hubert Howe Bancroft, *History of Nevada, Colorado and Wyoming, 1540-1888* (San Francisco, Calif.: History Co., 1890), p. 363n.

[5] Albert E. Reynolds, "Talk," 16 November 1920, transcribed by Vera Painter, Archives, La Junta Chapter, Daughters of the American Revolution (hereinafter cited as La Junta Chapter, DAR).

[6] The Cimmaron Cutoff shortened the route from Independence, Missouri, to Santa Fe to 840 miles. About 375 miles of this was the Cimmaron Cutoff itself. Traveling the cutoff "required that the mail stages be equipped for making night camps, which meant provisions of food, fodder, fuel, arms, and ammunitions. An available supply of buffalo or antelope meat, buffalo chips, and grass could not be counted on" (Morris F. Taylor, *First Mail West: Stagecoach Lines on the Santa Fe Trail* [Albuquerque: University of New Mexico Press, 1971]). Unless otherwise noted, all details on the mail routes to Santa Fe come from Taylor's book).

find a variety in a day's march of twenty miles."[7] The only other excitement on the trip was the first view of the Rocky Mountains. All travelers may not have cheered as Zebulon M. Pike's men, in November 1806, cheered for "the Mexican Mountains," but they all strained their eyes to the southwest to catch the first glimpse of the Spanish Peaks, and to the northwest, of Pikes Peak.[8]

While sight of the Rocky Mountains was important to the travelers on the trail, so was Bent's Old Fort, deserted or not, for they were accustomed to using it as an overnight stop. In 1851 Kit Carson and his party spent a night at the fort with Jesse Nelson, who, although he was only twenty-four years old, had made the trip on the Santa Fe Trail several times. This time he had paused in Missouri long enough to marry Kit's niece, Susan Carson. Then Jesse and his bride, and Kit's half-Indian daughter Adaline, and the "Old Man" (as Jesse called the forty-two-year-old Carson) headed west to deliver a herd of cattle over Raton Pass to Cimmaron, New Mexico. Kit seldom quarreled with the Indians, but on this trip the party was in real danger because Kit had forced an Indian to return a gold ring the Indian had appropriated from one of the girls. Kit was glad to "hole up" for the night in old Bent's Fort.[9]

Jesse and Susan (Carson) Nelson lived many years beyond 1851 when they camped for a night at the fort. Their great-great grandson, James Baldridge, sold his farm adjacent to the fort to the National Park Service about 125 years later.

Doubtless other wagon trains sought refuge behind those adobe walls, but in 1853 three well-equipped expeditions merely noted the fort and passed by. All three were surveying for a transcontinental railroad route. Edward F. Beale, an ex-Navy officer, commanded the first party. Heading for California to assume his duties as an Indian agent, Beale is best known to history as the man who imported camels from Africa to the American desert. Beale's young cousin, Gwinn W. Heap, kept the journal of the 1853 trip.

> May 31. Swarms of mosquitoes prevented much sleep . . . .
> Encamped three miles above Bent's Fort. We rode all through
> the ruins, which presented a strange appearance in these
> solitudes. A few years ago this post was frequented by numer-
> ous trappers and Indians, and at times exhibited a scene of
> wild confusion . . . . The adobe walls are still standing and are
> in many places of great thickness. They are covered with
> written messages from parties who had already passed here to
> their friends in the rear; they all stated that their herds were
> in good condition, and progressing finely.[10]

The second of the three railroad survey groups ignored the grafitti on the walls when they passed the old fort. Commanded by Captain John W. Gunnison, who was destined in a few weeks to be killed by the Paiute in Utah, a member of his party, E.G. Beckwith, reported:

> July 29. Between camp and Bent's Fort, grass was very abun-
> dant . . . . Bent abandoned his fort about four years ago, but
> not until he had destroyed it. Its adobe walls still stand in part
> only, with here and there a tower and chimney. Here, beyond
> all question, would be one of the most favorable points for a
> military post.[11]

---

[7] U.S., Congress, Senate, E.G. Beckwith, *Report of Explorations for a Route for a Pacific Railroad, by Captain J.W. Gunnison . . .,* in *Reports of Exploration and Surveys . . . in 1853-4,* vol. 2, 33d Cong., 2d sess., 1855, p. 27.

[8] Pikes Peak "looked like a cloud that never changed." The man who wrote that description lost enthusiasm for the view as, day after day, he rode west without reaching the mountains. "My impatience gradually subsided, as I became accustomed to the elephant long before reaching it" (Daniel E. Conner, *A Confederate in the Colorado Gold Fields* [Norman: University of Oklahoma Press, 1970], pp. 62-63).

[9] Jesse Nelson, "Tale of Our Oldest Pioneer," unidentified newspaper clipping, 26 November 1920, La Junta Chapter, DAR. This night is historically important because, more than a century later, Jesse Nelson's great-grandson, Jim Baldridge, who died about 1974, owned land near Bent's Old Fort, on which he raised "Black Angus cattle until it became necessary for him to sell the land to the government for a National Park. . . . The house and shed that are now [1975] here at the park were part of the Jim Baldridge ranch" (Gerald Garman, park ranger [historian], Bent's Old Fort National Historic Site, La Junta, Colorado, to Louisa Ward Arps, 15 September 1975).

[10] Gwinn W. Heap, *Central Route to the Pacific* (Philadelphia, Penn.: Lippincott, Grambo, 1854), pp. 24-25.

[11] Beckwith, *Report of Explorations,* p. 28.

John W. Gunnison   *John Charles Frémont*

The third railway survey party, under John Charles Frémont, a privately financed trip, chose winter to follow Gunnison's route across the San Juan Mountains. Frémont wanted to prove to himself and to his public that he could cross the Rocky Mountains in the winter, since his 1848 attempt had been disastrous. For supplies he stopped at Bent's New Fort, which William Bent had just built of stone six miles west of the present-day town of Lamar. The stop must have been purely business with no local gossip between the storekeepers and Frémont's men, because when Frémont later passed Bent's Old Fort, he thought that Indians had destroyed it.[12]

Upstream from Bent's Old Fort was the Pueblo settlement, which Indians did attack. The trading post was not only nearer the mountains than Bent's Old Fort, it was also nearer the Ute. In 1854 smallpox had decimated the Ute band. The tribe's unrest culminated on Christmas Day when they gained entry into the small fort and murdered all but four of the inhabitants.[13]

---

[12] Carvalho, *Incidents of Travel and Adventure in the Far West*, p. 134.

[13] LeRoy R. Hafen, "The Fort Pueblo Massacre and the Punitive Expedition against the Utes," *The Colorado Magazine* 4 (March 1927):50-51. For detailed information on Pueblo and the massacre,

*An 1853 sketch of the Wah-Ha-Ta-Gas or Spanish Peaks
by Richard Kern, an artist with the Gunnison survey.*

Following the attack on Pueblo, J.W. Atwood and John H. Tippetts and their families moved from the Saint Charles settlement down river to Bent's partly ruined old fort. Atwood had been near enough to Pueblo on that Christmas Day to see the Ute drive off the stock. When the Ute were gone, he helped bury the dead and then left for New Mexico to ask for assistance from the troops stationed there. During his absence, the Saint Charles settlement, which was about five miles down the Arkansas River from Pueblo, had also been attacked. So once again, in January 1855, though in a modest way, Bent's Old Fort became a trading post, operated by Atwood and Tippetts, who traded with the Cheyenne and the Arapaho instead of the Mountain Ute.[14]

In 1856 Jesse Nelson, the young man who had spent the night at the old fort in 1851 with his bride and Kit Carson, spent another night in the fort, which he remembered because he had "frozen his feet" there. If he actually meant *in* the fort, the accommodations offered by Atwood and Tippetts must have

see, Janet Lecompte, *Pueblo, Hardscrabble, Greenhorn: The Upper Arkansas, 1832-1856* (Norman: University of Oklahoma Press, 1978).

[14] LeRoy R. Hafen and Frank M. Young, "The Mormon Settlement at Pueblo, Colorado, during the Mexican War," *The Colorado Magazine* 9 (July 1932):134; Janet Lecompte, "Charles Autobees, V," ibid. 35 (January 1958):64.

been quite primitive.[15] Another frontiersman attracted to the fort in 1856 was the handsome Richens Lacy Wootton. Gossip reports that an attractive widow named Mary Anne Manning, traveling in an emigrant train from Pike County, Missouri, caught Wootton's eye when he was trading with the Indians at Bent's Old Fort, where he married her in a civil ceremony. A more dramatic tale is that he kidnapped her from Taos and brought her to live at Bent's Old Fort. They did not tarry long there, because Wootton was dispensing "Taos Lightning" on Christmas Day in 1858 to the gold seekers in Denver City.[16]

The Pikes Peak Gold Rush gave new life to Bent's Old Fort, as the well-worn Santa Fe Trail was the obvious way to get to the foot of the Rocky Mountains where the gold nuggets lay. Although the route soon had competition (the Platte River route from Omaha and the Smoky Hill route from Junction City, Kansas), the Kansas City papers played up the Arkansas River route as the water level route, the best natural road in the world. The latter trail passed by both Bent's New Fort and Bent's Old Fort and turned north at Pueblo up Fountain Creek over Mónument Hill Divide and down Cherry Creek into Denver. The newspapers seldom mentioned Indians or the possibility that they might be unfriendly.[17]

Besides the newspaper accounts, guidebooks and cheap little pamphlets were published and sold by the hundreds. Each guidebook contained advice on what equipment to take — one wagon with wooden axletree drawn by three yoke of oxen; told what supplies to take — for each person 20 pounds of coffee, 80 to 100 pounds of bacon; and warned about natural hazards — always cross streams in the evening before camping because they might be torrents in the morning. The guidebooks also listed mileage. On the Arkansas River route William Horner's guidebook specified: "Bent's Fort to Big Drunk Creek . . . 1-½ m., to Bent's Old Fort . . . 35-½ m." The descriptive passages were succinct, like Luke D. Tierney's comment, "I did not much notice the ruins of the old fort."[18]

---

[15] Nelson, "Tale of Our Oldest Pioneer," La Junta Chapter, DAR.

[16] The two main, and conflicting, sources for information about R.L. Wootton are: Howard L. Conrad, *Uncle Dick Wootton: The Pioneer Frontiersman of the Rocky Mountain Region* . . . (Chicago: Dibble & Co., 1890), and LeRoy R. Hafen, ed., *The Mountain Men and the Fur Trade of the Far West*, 10 vols. (Glendale, Calif.: Arthur H. Clarke Co., 1965), 3:397-411. Additional information on Wootton is found in Joseph J. Hill, *Ewing Young and the Fur Trade of the Far Southwest, 1822-1834* (Eugene, Oreg.: Cook Tiffany Co., 1923), p. 282; Jerome C. Smiley, *History of Denver, with Outlines of the Earlier History of the Rocky Mountain Country* (Denver: Times-Sun Publishing Co., 1901), p. 193.

[17] Taylor, *First Mail West*, p. 18.

[18] LeRoy R. Hafen, ed., *Pikes Peak Gold Rush Guidebooks of 1859*, Southwest Historical Series, vol.

The men who kept diaries of their trip along the Arkansas River were hardly more verbose than the guidebooks. In May 1858 William Green Russell from Georgia noted that "four or five men were living at Bent's Old Fort, who had considerable stock in trade goods and were dealing with the Indians." The William Larimer party noted: "We passed a band of Cheyenne Indians camping on the site of Col. Bent's old adobe fort, which now showed as nothing but a heap of tumbled walls." The next May at least one traveler disagreed with Larimer, for he wrote that "the highest walls that remained were about fourteen feet. The whole presented a formidable appearance."[19]

Up to the time of the gold rush, the Indians along the Arkansas River had only occasionally resented the white minority that was infiltrating their land. But after 1858 the Southern Cheyenne and the Arapaho, watching the long wagon trains traveling the river road, feared the invasion of too many whites. The Indians grew restless, the whites pleaded with Washington, D.C., for protection, and the army moved in to make it safe for white intruders to settle on the redman's land. By 1859 the army had decided that it needed a fort nearer the Rocky Mountains than Kansas, and army officials started to dicker with William Bent about using his new stone fort.

For Bent, this was a replay, for during the Mexican War, General Stephen W. Kearney's army had used his old adobe fort, their horses had ruined the grass near the fort, their weapons had scared away Bent's Indian customers, and, when the army had moved on, a quartermaster was left to supervise the army supplies stored in the fort. The government did offer to buy the fort, however, for what Bent considered a piddling sum. After the soldiers moved on, Bent moved out and built a new trading post about forty miles downstream from the old fort — above the flood plain of the Arkansas River — he knew the vagaries of that stream; and he built the fort of stone — he knew the upkeep required by adobe bricks.

Now the army was camped around his new stone fort, frightening Indian clients and dickering with Bent about buying this

---

9 (Glendale, Calif.: Arthur H. Clarke Co., 1941), pp. 101-2, 250; William B. Horner, *The Gold Regions of Kansas and Nebraska . . . Being a Complete Guide to the Gold Mines* (Chicago: W.H. Tobey & Co., 1859), pp. 54-55.

[19] F.W. Cragin interview with Theodore C. Dickson, Boulder, 1903, cited in Arthur Woodward, "Sidelights on Bent's Old Fort," *The Colorado Magazine* 33 (October 1956):281; Herman S. Davis, ed., *Reminiscences of General William Larimer and of His Son William H.H. Larimer* (Lancaster, Penn.: Privately printed, 1918), p. 74; Samuel D. Raymond, "Trip to Pike's Peak," Diary, Raymond Collection, Documentary Resources Department, State Historical Society of Colorado, Denver (hereinafter cited as SHSC).

second trading post. Willing to sell, he pointed out that the sixteen-foot high walls were made of stone, that the fort stood on top of an easily defended hill, and that its rooms included a fifty-four foot warehouse. Initially, the army leased the fort as a commissary building, agreeing to pay Bent sixty-five dollars a month rent. William Bent tried to collect this rent during the last nine months of his life. The army argued that they owed him nothing, because he had no title to the land on which the fort was built. Early in September 1860 army engineers chose a site for their own fort right on the river bank, downhill from Bent's New Fort. The fort was named Fort Wise, after the distinguished Henry A. Wise, at that time governor of Virginia.[20]

Although the soldiers from Fort Wise were now available for protection, the Cheyenne and the Arapaho had been persuaded to sign the Treaty of Fort Wise on 18 February 1861. While some of the chiefs repudiated this agreement, which confined their roaming to a specified area that included the site of Bent's Old Fort, this reservation did appear on the official map of the Territory of Colorado in November 1861.

In the spring of that year Bent's Old Fort once again became a busy stage station on the official mail route to Santa Fe. The United States postmaster general, tired of hearing how the mail had been destroyed on the Cimmaron Cutoff road by the Kiowa and the Comanche, decided to use what was known as the "Military Road," because Kearny had used it in 1846. This road crossed the river a little west of Bent's Old Fort, went southwest up Timpas Creek, down to Trinidad, and then crossed Raton Pass. The Missouri Stage Company renovated the old stations and built new ones, completing the route as far as Bent's Old Fort in the spring of 1861. The company advertised the service as the Kansas City, Santa Fe, and Canon City Fast Line.[21]

Colonel Jared L. Sanderson and his wife moved in to manage the Bent's Old Fort stage station, and by July 1861 meals were being served. In 1903 Colonel Sanderson remembered many details of the stage station at the old fort, the most astonishing of which was that he actually asked William Bent for permission to use the fort. He remembered that the walls were whitewashed anew, and that the kitchen and the dining room were on the

[20] "Place Names in Colorado (F)," *The Colorado Magazine* 18 (January 1941):30-31; Janet Lecompte, "Charles Autobees, VIII," ibid. 35 (July 1958):221-22; Julia S. Lambert, "Plain Tales of the Plains," *Trail* 8 (February 1916):9.

[21] Taylor, *First Mail West*, p. 78.

Jared L. Sanderson gave F.W. Cragin of Colorado Springs this sketch (artist unknown) of Bent's Old Fort as a stage station on the Mountain Branch of the Santa Fe Trail.

BENTS OLD FORT.

south side; two rooms were in use on the north side; and on the east, three rooms north of the old main gate and two rooms south of it were made habitable. The management kept extra wagons at the fort in case of a breakdown (the stages were literally wagons — the elegant red Concord stages came into use much later). Extra mules for the stages were always on hand and a blacksmith was in residence. Bent's Old Fort was considered to be, more or less, the half-way point, six hundred miles from Kansas City, four hundred from Santa Fe.[22]

---

[22] Sanderson remembered that he and his wife had lived at Bent's Old Fort for twenty years, a statement that "is open to serious challenge." Perhaps the Colonel's recollections of the details of the fort are equally spurious, but they are specific (Taylor, *First Mail West*, p. 123); one traveler reported that he arrived in time for a "regular pioneer supper" (*Canon City Times*, 11 July 1861).

The many miles that the Arkansas River lay from the Atlantic seaboard did not prevent news of the Civil War from flaming up the river like a prairie fire, and men declared for the Union or for the Confederacy as heatedly as if they lived in the shadow of Fort Sumter. Southern sympathizers among the soldiers stationed at Fort Wise defected. To help garrison the post, whose name was changed to Fort Lyon and whose total force in early 1862 had been reduced to thirty-nine men, Governor William Gilpin of Colorado Territory dispatched from Denver three companies of his recently recruited Colorado volunteer regiment, a tough group of men sometimes known as "Gilpin's Pet Lambs."[23] They were ordered to join the rest of the regiment in New Mexico. The first night out they camped near Bent's Old Fort. The peace of the camp was shattered when a courier galloped in with a dispatch from the commander of the Union forces in New Mexico, reporting that the Confederates had defeated his forces at Valverde on the Rio Grande and had captured nearly all of his field guns. Within a few hours, the troops moved away from Bent's Old Fort, to be part of a historic forced march to Fort Union, where they waited for two weeks, then helped save the West for the Union on 26 March 1862 at La Glorieta Pass, southeast of Santa Fe. Except for the excitement of that night when the Colorado Volunteers moved away from Bent's Old Fort, the only other direct effect the Civil War had on the old trading post turned stage station was that, during the days of the fight at Glorieta Pass, no regular stages carried the mail from Santa Fe.

Although Bent's Old Fort had been an official stage station on the mail route since 1861, its first official postmaster was not appointed until 4 June 1863.[24] Postmasters obtained their jobs through political pull, and Lewis Barnum had pull. His brother was at one time a partner in the stage company, and his bride was the niece of Colonel Albert G. Boone, the Indian agent who had succeeded William Bent. Twenty-seven-year-old Lewis Barnum married Emma Boone at Booneville (present-day Boone), where Colonel Boone, his brother, and their families lived in true southern comfort, even though their little settle-

---

23 When news that Governor Wise of Virginia had declared for the Confederacy, the fort's name was changed to Fort Lyon in honor of General Nathaniel Lyon of the Union army, who had died in the battle of Wilson's Creek, Missouri, in August 1861 (Arthur J. Flynn, "Furs and Forts of the Rocky Mountain West," *The Colorado Magazine* 9 [March 1932]:56).

24 U.S., Postmaster General, "Post Office Records, 1863-1873," Washington, D.C.; William H. Bauer, et al, *Colorado Postal History: The Post Office* (Crete, Nebr.: J-B Publishing Co., 1971), p. 21.

The present-day town of Boone, on the Arkansas River below Pueblo, was started by and named for Missourian Albert G. Boone.

ment sat on the lonely banks of the Arkansas River about fifty miles above Bent's Old Fort. Because his bride was not used to roughing it, surely Lewis Barnum must have prepared good quarters for her in the partially wrecked old fort. Perhaps at least one of the many coats of plaster, "quite spectacular" in red, yellow, or white, which archaeologists found traces of in Room S2, dates from Emma Boone Barnum's day.[25]

As the postmaster's lady she had no duties connected with feeding the transients and the employees of the station. That job was taken over by a Baptist minister, the Reverend Barzillai M. Adams, who had fled from his Missouri farm because of the Civil War. He and a friend, James Cooper, managed to outfit an old worn-out wagon for their wives and children, hoping that they "would appear too pitiable and insignificant to be molested." At Westport, the two men got a job driving a wagon to Las Vegas, New Mexico. "It was pretty hard to send the women and children back to nothing, but they accepted the situation very cheerfully," wrote the Reverend Mr. Adams.

> I shouldered my whip and drove six yoke of oxen to a sixty hundred wagon very cheerfully if not gracefully. This occurred the last of October, 1862. We reached Bent's Old Fort about Christmas. There the train had to be divided. About half

[25] Herbert W. Dick, "The Excavation of Bent's Fort, Otero County, Colorado," *The Colorado Magazine* 33 (July 1956):192.

of the cattle could not go through without recruiting. I was one left with the weak cattle, where we remained until late in the winter when the cattle were sufficiently recruited to go on. We made the trip alright and I returned to Bent's Fort in March, I think.

Bent's Fort was a stage station of the old overland stage company, Barlow Barnum & Co. at that time. It was the junction with Kansas City, Denver, and Santa Fe. It was general headquarters for agents and conductors, drivers, etc., thus congregating at times from ten to twenty men connected with the road. Besides there was a great deal of travel on the road of soldiers and citizens, thus making it a place of importance.

I had seen all this while I was in camp below, and felt that I would like to be a partner in the institution. I got back there very early in the morning. I knew not where I should go from there. I could not go back home in safety. But while we were preparing breakfast by our campfire the proprietor came to us and offered me forty dollars per month to cook for him. That was just what I wanted.

I told the boys they might do their own cooking after that. I engaged and went to work immediately. I formed acquaintance with the parties interested in the road. Made myself very useful and obliging as was my nature and more than that with the women help. They said there was a great change for the better. It was not long before the proprietor heard hints that I would suit this station pretty well and he concluded he had better get along without me. Accordingly he paid me off.
Next morning I got on the stage and had a free ride sixty miles up to my old friend, Col. A.G. Boone of long acquaintance, who was also keeping a station. It was there I first saw Barlow, and it was there that Barnum and Barlow gave me charge of Bent's Old Fort. I think I was put in possession about the first of June. For several weeks until the family came I was landlord, cook, and dishwasher. We had no beds to make. It was the rule for every fellow to carry his bed with him. If he had no bed he was shown the hay rick.

By and by the family came, or a part of them, for they had to come on that same stage line and had to be divided. They could bring very little with them in the way of clothing, bedding, tableware, etc. But by degrees changes were made, for instance, a table cloth was spread over the rough board table. A few dishes were added occasionally, until finally the place was considered on the road "Bon Ton." Although we were now forty miles from an American family [Fort Lyon] and sixty to the second, Col. Boone's, we felt quite at ease . . . .

The business at the station increased rapidly. We had enough to do to keep us out of mischief. We only had occasional preaching, but observed the Sabbath as well as we could and exerted a general influence for good over those about us . . . .

The first year of our stay at Bent's Fort was upon the whole pleasant and quiet with some success financially. The proprietors of the road were nice men to deal with. The men employed were agreeable and pleasant, thus making our home rather desirable. The many comers and goers supplied the lack of neighbors.[26]

Three of these "comers and goers," as reported by Mr. Adams, were also ministers, Episcopal clergy taking the long journey from Denver to Santa Fe. One was Bishop Joseph C. Talbot, the energetic missionary bishop of the Northwest who called himself "The Bishop of All Outdoors." The other two were a Mr. Rich, a delicate New Yorker, and a Mr. DeMora, brought along because he could speak Spanish. Neither of them was as hardy as the large, forty-eight-year-old bishop, who was making his third trip west from Omaha. They traveled under orders from their eastern superiors who had written Bishop Talbot that as long as he was going to Denver, why not drop down to Santa Fe. Unable to explain to Easterners the many miles involved in western geography, the three set out from Denver on 17 June 1863.

The crowded stage stopped only for meals, including a two-hour stay at Colonel Boone's where they were entertained "in the style of true Kentucky hospitality." (The bishop had lived in Kentucky and knew that Colonel Boone was Daniel Boone's grandson.) In his journal for 19 June the bishop wrote:

> We left this comfortable home about sundown and arrived at Bent's Fort at 6 a.m. Not a military, but an old trading post, as these strong "adobe" buildings were erected in early times for protection against the Indians. We have several [posts] and they are all quite formidable in size and appearance.
>
> Here we lie over 24 hours for the coach from the east for Santa Fe. It is a very uncomfortable place — the dirt floors, the hard living and the bedbugs, together present an array of inconvenience — appalling to my New York brother, and though nothing new to me, not greatly to be desired . . . . The Santa Fe coach from the east has come in . . . . The station at Bent's Old Fort is kept by Mr. Adams, a Baptist preacher, who does his best, but will be able to make things more comfortable when his wife and daughter arrive. They are expected every day.
>
> Saturday 20th. We were full of guests at the Fort last night and though a bed was offered me, I preferred to give it up to

[26] Before the Civil War Mr. Adams lived on a prosperous farm south of Independence, Missouri, near Harrisonville. His "Autobiography" paints a picture of his experiences at Bent's Old Fort and later as the Baptist minister at Canon City. B.M. Adams, "Autobiography," typescript, SHSC (original manuscript in the State Historical Society of Wisconsin, Madison).

DeMora and take my blanket in the coach outside. The night was passed very uncomfortably, even there, as I was obliged to take a very constrained position and got little sleep. At 3 a.m. I was awakened by preparations to start the coach I had taken and had to "turn out." Next I took a mail bag in the Fort. This was soon called for and at last I spread a blanket on the floor when I was soon aroused with the information that breakfast would be ready as soon as I.

I am sure that it would both surprise and amuse our eastern friends to see the "stopping over" camping in such a place as this — some had beds and bugs — some the floor — and quite a number the ground or straw in the corral, the latter perhaps the best of all for they could breathe the free air while they were at the same time free from the phlebotomising propensities of the unmentionable insects inside.

Notwithstanding these trivial discomforts, my friends all unused to it are cheerful this morning and DeMora drowns in a happy whistle the pain of what he calls a chronic bite between his shoulders.

Six p.m. We are over the river and off for Santa Fe but what a trial to get off: never have I seen such imposition upon passengers as that practiced by the Kansas City and Santa Fe Stage Co. There is no limit either as to passengers or express matter and the result is that as in our own case, they pack us in for a ride of four hundred miles without the slightest chance even to stretch our legs, etc. In this connection I cannot but record the infinite patience and good temper of their excellent conductor, Mr. Smith, gentlemanly and accommodating in a very remarkable degree — he does what he can to redeem the concern from the unmeasured condemnation of every passenger of our company. What a company! We find ourselves fellow passengers with four or five of the most terrible profane and unclean of men. The whole of this night, they were drinking to excess, blaspheming, and singing obscene songs to the utter disgust of their fellow passengers and to our great sorrow of heart. I rode the entire night upon the driver's box, without sleep of course. Poor DeMora was greatly afflicted by the profanity within, but Mr. Rich slept through it all.[27]

Travel around Bent's Old Fort became more difficult when the seriousness of the white-Indian situation heightened in late 1864. Soon after the Sand Creek massacre on 29 November 1864, Adams left the fort to settle near Canon City, so probably no minister was at the fort on 21 June 1865 to officiate at the burial of "Edward Dorris, aged 31 years, 2ms," whose tombstone still marks his grave outside the walls of the reconstructed Bent's Old Fort. That summer Dorris was not the only white person buried under the grass of the Colorado plains. In revenge

[27]   Joseph C. Talbot, "Diary of Trip to Colorado, 1863," in Louisa Ward Arps, ed., "The Church Marks the Centennial," *Colorado Episcopalian* (January 1961).

for Sand Creek the Indians made 1865 hideous for white settlers and travelers, starting with the destruction of Julesburg in the northeast corner of Colorado Territory in January.[28]

In southeastern Colorado the United States government was able to collect enough Southern Cheyenne and Arapaho by October to sign a treaty that spread a semblance of peace over the Arkansas River valley. The agreement was the first indication that the Indians might accept their fate of being herded on to reservations in the Indian Territory (present-day Oklahoma). Although the actual departure was piecemeal and dilatory, the Treaty of the Little Arkansas on 14 October 1865 started the movement south. Article V of the treaty, however, made an exception:

> At the special request of the Cheyenne and Arrapahoe [*sic*] Indians, parties to this treaty, the United States agree to grant, by patent in fee-simple, to the following-named persons, all of whom are related to the Cheyennes or Arrapahoes [*sic*] by blood, to each an amount of land equal to one section of six hundred and forty acres, viz: [Here follows a list of thirty-one names.] . . . . Said lands to be selected under the direction of the Secretary of the Interior, from the reservation established by the 1st article of their treaty of February 18, A.D. 1861.[29]

Were the lands granted at the "special request" of the Cheyenne and the Arapaho, or were they the request of influential white men, such as William Bent and John Prowers, who had no intention of having their Indian wives and half-Indian children herded down to Indian Territory? Article V awarded the Bent and the Prowers kin specific sections of 640 acres of land north of the Arkansas River, land which previously had been awarded by the 1861 Treaty of Fort Wise to the two Indian nations in general.[30]

The thirty-one sections of land granted to the blood relatives of the Cheyenne and the Arapaho were known as "beef steak claims" because of their irregular shape, irregular because the south line of each claim was on the Arkansas River. The land awarded to Julia Bent, William Bent's youngest child, was Claim 13, west of Claim B, which was awarded to Jenny Lind

---

[28] Adams, "Autobiography"; Mrs. C.F. Parker, "Old Julesburg and Fort Sedgwick," *The Colorado Magazine* 7 (July 1930):145-46.

[29] Charles J. Kappler, ed., *Indian Affairs, Laws and Treaties*, 3 vols. (Washington, D.C.: Government Printing Office, 1904), 2:889.

[30] Ibid.; Lillian B. Shields, "Relations with the Cheyennes and Arapahoes in Colorado to 1861," *The Colorado Magazine* 4 (August 1927):153-54.

Amache, a Cheyenne, married John Prowers, after whom Prowers County is named. Her father, Ochinee, was killed at the battle of Sand Creek.

Crocker, and east of Claim 14, which was awarded to "A-ma-che, alias Amache Prowers," the wife of cattleman John Prowers. Bent's Old Fort was on Julia Bent's section.[31]

No matter who owned the land on which Bent's Old Fort stood, life went on as usual at the stage station. With the Indians seeking revenge for the Sand Creek massacre, Lewis Barnum may have decided that the risk was too great to keep his wife at the old fort; also he was advancing in the management of the stage company. A new postmaster was appointed on 20 October 1865, Edward W. Lansing, who stayed only that winter, and was replaced by James W. Cooper on 18 April 1866. Perhaps this was the same James Cooper who had come from Missouri with the Reverend Barzillai M. Adams. Cooper served almost two years, though his postal duties could not have been arduous. Only two mail stages, heavily guarded, left Fort Union each month, one using the Bent's Old Fort route, the other using the Cimmaron Cutoff.[32]

---

[31] M.S. Lessig, Surveyor General of Colorado, "Map of Indian Claims . . . of lands reserved to mixed bloods under the provisions of the Treaty . . . October 14, 1865," Record Group 49, Colorado 6B, National Archives, Washington, D.C. Julia Bent's mother was Yellow Woman, William Bent's second Cheyenne wife. That autumn of 1865, could the award of 640 acres of land have comforted Julia Bent when she learned that Pawnee scouts, hired by the army on the Powder River in Wyoming, had danced in triumph around five Cheyenne scalps, one of which was her mother's? (Lavender, *Bent's Fort*, p. 362).

[32] Taylor, *First Mail West*, pp. 96, 106-7.

Divergent opinions of the stage facilities appeared in newspapers in January 1866. One reporter noted that the company had converted the fort into "a very complete and comfortable station," and gave special praise to Arthur Hill, who had charge of the coach from Denver. The other reporter disliked the stage company's coaches, the weather, and the fort, but he was pleased when Hill announced the arrival of the stage at each station by blowing "a fish horn solo."[33]

To add to the misery of living through the Indian troubles, the spring of 1867 brought torrential rains. The flooded river wiped out old Fort Lyon, proving that the army should have heeded William Bent who had built his new post on higher

A Robert Lindneux painting depicts Fort Lyon on the Arkansas River with Bent's New Fort on the hill above.

ground. According to a visitor late that summer, Fort Lyon, "abandoned only three months, looked like an ancient ruin infested with rats and rattlesnakes."[34]

The night of the flood the soldiers at Fort Lyon retreated to safer ground and put up their campaign tents in soggy discomfort. The very next day an officer took some men up river to locate a place to rebuild the fort. He picked a site just north and across the river from the present-day town of Las Animas. In a few days the whole contingent marched to the site, and, with

[33] Ibid., pp. 109-10.
[34] William A. Bell, *New Tracks in North America: A Journey of Travel and Adventure . . . during 1867-68* (New York: Scribner Welford & Co., 1870), p. 76.

various civilian employees, started to erect a new fort, retaining the name of Fort Lyon.[35]

Among the civilian employees who moved upstream with the soldiers was the sutler, a word used then for what army men today call the man who runs the Post Exchange or PX. The sutler, Albert E. Reynolds and his partner John Thatcher, later to become an important banker at Pueblo, contracted to furnish lime for building the new fort and constructed a short ditch from the river to their kiln. Later, Reynolds took delight in telling his family that he had built the very first building at the new Fort Lyon.[36]

With Fort Lyon rising on the north side of the river, the year 1867 saw a lessening of the hotel business at Bent's Old Fort. Two cattlemen, Daniel W. Holbrook and Philip Lander, bought the stage station from William Bent for their range headquarters. Holbrook became the postmaster, soon succeeded by his partner Lander. They still fed stage passengers, but not as many since a direct stage now ran from Denver to Pueblo to Trinidad to connect with the Santa Fe stages from the east. Denver passengers no longer needed to jolt the boring miles down the Arkansas River east from Pueblo to connect with the Santa Fe stage at Bent's Old Fort.[37]

In 1920, when Reynolds was eighty-years-old, he remembered how the stage station at Bent's Old Fort looked when he was twenty-seven. "I have driven into that place on the stage a number of times. They used to come in and drive around the Fort, coming in from the westerly side, into the enclosure, and my recollection is that I was first there in 1867." He refuted the statement that "there was a big gate there, sixty feet wide, or something, covered with sheet iron. Nothing of the kind . . . . That four horse stage would swing right in there . . . a wide opening."

Reynolds went on to say that the fort was "built as any Mexican would build his house, built to be headquarters for Bent, a place to live for himself and his family and his clerks and people of that kind who were trading with the Indians . . . . It

---

[35] W.B. Vickers, *History of the Arkansas Valley, Colorado* (Chicago: O.L. Baskin & Co., 1881), p. 843.

[36] Albert E. Reynolds, "Family Papers."

[37] If money actually passed between the cattlemen and William Bent, this was the only cash on record that Bent ever realized on his property. No mention was made of Julia Bent, who was supposed to have been given the land by the Treaty of the Little Arkansas of 1865. In April 1867 a Jewish merchant in Denver, Abraham Jacobs, put up the money to run a stage line directly from Denver to Trinidad. Taylor, *First Mail West*, pp. 128, 138.

A.E. Reynolds (left) and Mahlon Thatcher, a Pueblo banker whose brother, John, was Reynold's partner in 1868 at New Fort Lyon.

was never built to fight Indians . . . . They came out here with peaceable intent."[38]

By 1870, three years following Reynolds first visit to the fort, Lander had acquired a new partner, an extra-large man named M.B. Price. His obvious interest in food was reflected in the meal that he served to W.R. Thomas, a Denver newspaperman. In March, Thomas rode a stage pulled by five mules hitched in a triangle, two at the wheel and three abreast in the lead. From King's Ferry (present-day La Junta), which by this time boasted a bridge, the mules ran seven miles in one hour on the north side of the river to Bent's Old Fort "where an excellent dinner was provided" for Thomas and others who were visiting the fort.[39]

Later that summer Peter G. Scott, destined to become one of the first schoolteachers in that part of the valley, kept a journal of his trip to Bent's Old Fort. At Kit Carson, which was on the Kansas Pacific railroad line to Denver, Scott started south with a wagon train at seven o'clock in the morning. Within one-half

[38] Reynolds, "Talk," La Junta Chapter, DAR.
[39] *Denver Daily Rocky Mountain News*, 12 April 1870.

hour, the travelers came to the Big Sandy bottoms, where the drivers hitched nine yoke of oxen to one wagon, "but it took a great deal of shouting in their own peculiar Mexican lingo, and a great deal of cracking these terrible bullock whips before we got through .... These fellows can swing their whips round their heads and strike a terrible blow."

> Friday 26th. Got to the Arkansas River a little before sundown and camped beside Bent's Fort, an old Indian trading post. The fort is built of sundried brick, in a square with houses leaned up against the wall on the inside. The wall is about 10 feet high and the roofs of the shanties slope inward. The stables occupy one side of the square. Several lines of stage cross here and there is a P.O. in which I put a letter. There is a large drove of horses and mules and 400 cattle belonging to Price who lives at the fort. In the inside there is a large yard where they run in the stage, etc. The roofs of the houses are made of poles covered with a thin stratum of clay and not calculated to hold out water I should think.[40]

In 1954 this same Peter G. Scott, who had come to Colorado in 1870 to "recover from a persistent cold," remembered M.B. Price, the proprietor of Bent's Old Fort who was later prominent in Bent County politics, as a "large good-natured gentleman, in fact he weighed over three hundred pounds in his shirt sleeves. When he first saw me come in he looked up and said 'lunger!' That was the first time I had been called by that name, but I guess it fitted .... He showed me around, ... told me very little repairs had been done to the place, and that to the roof only, and that I was seeing it just as Bent and the Indians with whom he was trading had left it."[41]

By early 1872 Julia Bent was living at the fort, for she had received legal title to the property on 20 September 1870. The post office and the accommodations for travelers were still there, and cattlemen continued to run cattle on her land. On 10 April 1872 Julia sold her section of land to John W. Prowers, who was amassing a large cattle spread along the river. He already had Claim 14, just east of Julia's, which had been deeded to his Cheyenne wife Amache. He probably acquired Edmund Guerrier's claim also, for about this time Julia Bent married Edmund Guerrier, and they moved to Oklahoma.[42]

[40] Peter G. Scott, "Diary of a Freighting Trip from Kit Carson to Trinidad in 1870," *The Colorado Magazine* 8 (July 1931): 147, 150-51.

[41] Peter G. Scott, *La Junta Tribune-Democrat*, 10 July 1954.

[42] "Warranty Deed between Julia Bent and John H. Prowers," no. 6204, 27 September 1862, Albert E. Reynolds, "Family Papers." The town of Geary, northwest of Oklahoma City, Okla., bears the anglicized name of Edmond Guerrier, whose father was a French Canadian plainsman.

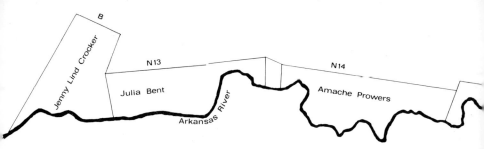

*A drawing based on an 1870 map by M.S.
Lessig, surveyor general of Colorado, showing
three of the claims, including Julia Bent's (N13), daughter
of William Bent and his second wife Yellow Woman.*

According to the deed of transfer, Prowers acquired Julia Bent's Claim 13 "in consideration of $3200" (or $5.00 per acre). Scott, the one-time "lunger," remembered the deal this way: "At this time the old fort belonged to Julia Bent, and in the summer of 1872 she sold it to John W. Prowers and I helped deliver the cattle that she received for the place."[43]

Julia's departure cut the last cord connecting the old fort with the family of its builder. Other changes occurred rapidly. The Kansas Pacific railroad's branch line from Kit Carson arrived in West Las Animas in time to ship the huge stacks of hides and, later, bones, accumulating from the slaughter of the great southern buffalo herd. No definite date marks the last meal served to travelers stopping at Bent's Old Fort, but it may have been about 2 December 1873 when Walter H. Brown, last postmaster, closed the United States Post Office. However, the fort was far from deserted, for the next year a railroad guide book reported its population as forty.[44]

It is doubtful that these people were paying rent to owner John W. Prowers, but he was utilizing his fort as a line camp and sometimes as roundup headquarters for his cowboys who were tending his cattle in the western part of his domain. The old fort made a good corral, or "kraal," as one cowboy spelled the word. John W. Prowers shipped thousands of Herefords to eastern markets. By 1880 he controlled forty miles of river banks, and he had thrown eighty miles of barbed wire fence around one parcel of land. All of the land did not belong to him, but cattlemen were controlling the grazing land by fencing the water sources. Into this vast grazing empire filtered the farmers, homesteading Indian lands north of the river and, to the south, land that had been claimed by the Vigil and St. Vrain Land

---

[43] Scott, *La Junta Tribune-Democrat*, 10 July 1954; *see also* Scott, "John W. Prowers, Bent County Pioneer," *The Colorado Magazine* 7 (September 1930):183-87.

[44] *Routes of Travel in Colorado: A Hand-book of Information* . . . (Denver: *Rocky Mountain News*, 1874), appendix, p. iii.

Grant. Perhaps it was just as well that Prowers died in 1884, the year the Fort Lyon Canal appropriated its first water from the Arkansas River, the beginning of Colorado's most extensive irrigation system, and the year before 1885 when President Cleveland ordered the removal of all illegal fences on the open cattle ranges.[45] As the fenced range disappeared so did Bent's Old Fort. A.E. Reynolds noted that "Bent's Old Fort began to 'crumble' when the country roundabout began to be cut up into ranches. The ranchers carried away the adobe bricks by the wagonload and then used them in construction of their houses and barns." Another man wrote that the farmers "spirited away" the bricks. Still another, less diplomatic, used the word "stole."[46]

A. E. Reynolds had a long time interest in Bent's Old Fort, indeed a vested interest, since he owned its site for the last twenty-one years of his life. He had come to Fort Lyon as its sutler in 1867, and after careers in Oklahoma and Texas as sutler, hide collector, freighter, and rancher, he became a mining magnate in Colorado. By 1900 he had amassed enough money to return to his first love — the Arkansas River valley, where he bought or leased a reputed 6,000 acres of land, which included water rights in the Fort Lyon Canal and a parcel of 300 acres on which stood Bent's Old Fort. Reynolds wrote that "John Prowers' heirs sold [the 300 acres] to me. Marshall, their name is, and they are at Las Animas."[47]

In acquiring farm land Reynolds was not only returning to the Fort Lyon area, where he had started his Colorado career, but also to his earliest occupation, for he had been raised on a farm near Buffalo, New York. Although he hired managers for his farm and rented out portions of the acreage to small farmers,

---

[45] Perhaps the best evidence of the use of the fort as a corral lies in the earth. In 1954 Herbert W. Dick sunk a core in the floor of one of the north rooms. He estimated that during the stage station period the room acquired two inches of packed dirt, but during the cattle period seven inches of fill accumulated, composed of manure and cow bones mixed with disintegrated adobe (Dick, "Excavation of Bent's Fort," p. 189); Scott, "John W. Prowers," p. 185; William R. White, "Illegal Fencing on the Colorado Range," *The Colorado Magazine* 22 (Spring 1975).

[46] Josiah Ward, "Abandonment of the Historic Fort: Interview with A.E. Reynolds," *Denver Post,* 8 February 1920.

Archaeologists are still looking for adobe bricks bound with wool. David Lavender found evidence of this. He wrote that perhaps over one hundred Mexicans were brought from Taos to build the fort and "also from Taos came dozens of wagonloads of course, cap Mexican wool to use as binding for the mud" (Lavender, *Bent's Fort,* p. 138). Also, H.L. Lubers, in the address he gave at the dedication of the DAR marker on the site of Bent's Old Fort in 1912, stated that "Wool being cheap he [Charles Bent] sent some wagon-loads of Mexican wool to be mixed with the clay of the brick to give them greater strength and life" (*Las Animas Bent County Democrat,* 20 September 1912).

[47] Reynolds, "Talk," La Junta Chapter, DAR. The deed from Thomas H. Marshall to Reynolds, 20 February 1900, Otero County Land Records, La Junta, Colorado.

he could intelligently supervise and advise the agricultural operations. Not only that, he could, and did, experiment. Recognizing the fruit growing possibilities of the Arkansas River valley, he planted a large orchard of cherry trees and watched them mature until the year they bore plentiful fruit. Just before picking time, a hail storm ruined not only the fruit but also the tender trees. Their skeletons, like that of Bent's Old Fort, stood for years.[48]

While only a specter of its early years of glory, Bent's Old Fort was not totally forgotten. On a hot afternoon on 5 September 1912, a splendid affair took place on the north bank of the Arkansas River. Along with the chapters in Missouri, Kansas, and New Mexico, the Colorado chapters of the Daughters of the American Revolution had been erecting markers along the Santa Fe Trail in their own state. Now they were ready to unveil the gray granite plaque at the site of Bent's Old Fort. They had approached A.E. Reynolds, owner of the site, who not only heartily agreed with their historic gesture but paid for the marker.[49]

Reynolds was prepared to go even further, as the local newspaper reported. "Some time ago he made known his intention of presenting the site to Otero County to be made into a park that travelers on the Trail might stop at least for a time to do honor to this historical place." When this announcement was made at the celebration, the feud between Otero County and Bent County surfaced, a feud that had been seething since 1889 when the state surveyors, dividing up the much too large original Bent County, had left Bent's Old Fort in Otero County, just west of the new Bent County line. Mayor John C. Davidson of Las Animas (Bent County) rose to remind the audience that

> Bent County was named in memory of the builder of the fort, that his [Bent's] granddaughter [Mrs. H.L. Lubers], who had always lived in Las Animas, was present to unveil the monument, and that many of his descendants still lived in Bent County. We were more interested in the ceremonies in progress today than were the people of Otero County, but that we would consider it a pleasure and part of our duty to give such aid and assistance in seeing in remembrance these early pioneers and the preservation of this historic place.

---

[48] Interview with Mrs. George Garrey (Anna Reynolds Morse Garrey), March 1975, Denver.

[49] Reynolds was active in trying to preserve Colorado history, and supported the efforts of the DAR in its work throughout the state (Secretary, Colorado DAR, to Reynolds, 21 March 1921, "Family Papers"). The year on the marker is 1910, not 1912, the year of the ceremony. Margaret Long, *The Santa Fe Trail* (Denver: By the Author, 1954), pp. vii, 163-165.

On 5 September 1912 nearly two hundred people
gathered at the site of the fort for the dedication
ceremonies of the DAR marker. A genuine Overland
stagecoach, driven by old-timer Jimmie Brown,
transported fourteen passengers, including A.E.
Reynolds (sitting at the edge of the roof). Mrs. Freeman C.
Rogers, Colorado State Regent of the DAR (right), A.E.
Reynolds, and possibly the granddaughter of William
Bent, Mrs. H.L. Lubers, gathered at the marker for their
photograph.

This touched a responsive chord and a county commissioner of Otero County said that it would be a pleasure to have Bent County cooperate. A.E. Reynolds remarked that if it was agreeable he would convey as many acres of ground to the two counties as they should decide was necessary to the purpose.[50] Despite the politeness displayed in the speeches given at the dedication of the marker in 1912, the two counties failed to cooperate and Reynolds did not deed any land. Virtually nothing was accomplished until 1920 when the La Junta Chapter of the DAR in Otero County, with the support of A.E. Reynolds, made some progress toward preserving the old fort as well as enhancing the site. Organized in 1913, shortly after the unveiling of the monument, the chapter officially received the fort site from A.E. Reynold's daughter on 8 February 1926, five years following his death. Seventy-seven years after its abandonment by William Bent, "in consideration of $1.00," the La Junta Chapter of the Daughters of the American Revolution received the deed to Bent's Old Fort from Mrs. Anna Reynolds Morse, conveying "4.41 acres of land and, more or less, together with all of the Capital Stock of the Fort Lyon Canal Company."[51] Between 1912 and 1920 the fort site was a dry field marked only by a few crumbled adobes, Edward Dorris's gravestone, and the DAR marker.

The author of DENVER IN SLICES *and numerous books and articles dealing with Colorado history, LOUISA WARD ARPS received a Historic Denver Annual Award in 1971. A University of Colorado alumna and a graduate of the Library School of the New York City Public Library, she is a member of the Colorado Authors League, the Denver Woman's Press Club, and several other Denver and Colorado organizations.*

---

[50] *Las Animas Bent County Democrat,* 20 September 1912.

[51] "Warranty Deed, Bent's Fort Land and Cattle Company, a corporation, to La Junta Chapter of the Daughters of the American Revolution, a corporation," no. 186063, 8 February 1926, Otero County Land Records, La Junta, Colorado.

From Ruin to
Reconstruction, 1920-1976

BY MERRILL J. MATTES

On 27 May 1975 the federal government began the authentic reconstruction of Bent's Old Fort on the Santa Fe Trail. On 5 July there was a simple dedication ceremony attendant upon laying the first adobe brick. After the laying of several hundred thousand more bricks, on 25 July 1976 the State of Colorado joined the National Park Service in dedicating the completed reconstruction project — Bent's Old Fort — looking as much like the famous original as historical and archaeological research and architectural ingenuity allowed. This was 155 years after 1821, the time of the first American caravan to Santa Fe; 143 years after 1833, the date that most historians accept as the original year of construction of the fort by William Bent and associates; and 127 years after 1849, the date of the abandonment of the trading post.

The year 1976 seemed particularly appropriate for the occasion because it marked both the state's Centennial and the nation's Bicentennial. Since Bent's Old Fort is acknowledged to be the first Anglo-American settlement in Colorado as well as a pivotal factor in the early history of the whole American Southwest, there could have been no celebration of this occasion more significant than the resurrection of this unique mud bastion on

the Arkansas River, the one-time outpost of American civilization in the western wilderness and a vivid reminder of our frontier heritage.

There are acres of print, in books and articles, that dwell on the history of the fort, involving chapters on exploration, the fur trade, the military conquest of Mexico and California, and a parade of colorful characters. Almost nothing has been written about the far less glamorous period of recent history when Arkansas River valley citizens struggled to save remnants of the old fort, which had been marked in 1912 by the La Junta Chapter of the Daughters of the American Revolution, or the succeeding periods of state and federal custodianship with the flickering hopes for eventual reconstruction that finally were fulfilled. This, therefore, is the story of Bent's Old Fort from 1920, when the site was taken over by a local chapter of the DAR to the climax years 1972 through 1976, when the National Park Service, with the timely help of key Colorado citizens and the Colorado congressional delegation, was able to "put it all together."

The La Junta Chapter of the Daughters of the American Revolution was organized on 24 November 1913. However, it was not until 23 September 1924 that this group filed a Certificate of Incorporation "for educational and patriotic purposes," one of said purposes being "to mark the suitable monuments historical points and places and to preserve and protect historical sites and buildings," likewise "to make, hold or receive the title to real and personal property by donation, purchase, or otherwise." The circumstance that precipitated this action was the discovery that this organization could not legally own the site of Bent's Old Fort until it was incorporated, even though it had accepted the site in 1920 as a supposed donation by ranch owner Albert E. Reynolds. The Warranty Deed of the Bent's Fort Land and Cattle Company to the La Junta Chapter, DAR, dated 8 February 1926, was recorded on 5 March of that year.[1] Technically, therefore, 1926 marks the beginning of DAR own-

---

[1] All material relating to the DAR phase was supplied by the La Junta Chapter through the intercession of the area NPS Superintendent John R. Patterson. That portion of the material evidently gleaned from minutes of the chapter meetings or other chapter records are hereinafter referred to as La Junta Chapter, DAR. Mrs. J.R. (Marjorie Allen) White is identified as the principal contributor, with assistance by Mrs. Lee Strain, Mrs. F.A. Rowden, and others. Mrs. White served as regent in 1963, celebrated by the La Junta Chapter, DAR, as its Golden Anniversary, which coincided with the first year of NPS occupation of Bent's Fort National Historic Site.

Signers of the incorporation document are identified as Gladys E. Halsey, Birtie Morrison, Carrie Allen Rice, Ethel Whitcomb Hutchinson, and Laura Burshears, La Junta, DAR Register of Deeds, Book 275, p. 62, City and County of Denver, Denver.

ership and the organized effort to preserve and, hopefully, to restore the fort. However, for practical purposes this effort began six years earlier when the DAR chapter innocently believed that it had acquired the place and then proceeded to take steps accordingly.

It is not clear which DAR officers or members first conceived the idea of taking on this fort as a project, or exactly when they conceived it, but things were in motion as early as April 1920 when, at a regular monthly meeting, Mary Jenkins Hart and Harriett Grant Bragg were appointed as a committee "to see the County Commissioners, also Mr. Reynolds, regarding the former promise of a road leading into old Fort Bent." At the ensuing May meeting these two ladies "gave a splendid report of the results obtained," presumably a promise by the county commissioners to grade an entrance road at an early date. Other ideas blossomed forth — that high school pupils be asked to "submit designs for the marking of an entrance to Bent's Fort," that schoolchildren of all ages be asked for five cents each to help improve the fort, and that a Bent's Old Fort Day be proclaimed "for the purposes of carrying on the work." All of the motions were carried.[2]

At the October meeting of the DAR Chapter, A.E. Reynolds and George Williams were present to "talk over improvements" at the site, and the treasurer reported a total of $135.74 in the Bent's Fort Fund. And, on 11 November 1920 at a special meeting held at the home of Judge and Mrs. M.F. Miller, the fort site and access strip "was given [to] the chapter by Mr. Reynolds and Mr. Williams," according to the La Junta Chapter records. The 1920 "gift" of the fort site and access strip may have been a verbal promise rather than a legal document. Neither Reynolds nor his foreman Williams owned the land as individuals, for on 10 January 1920 the Bent's Fort Land and Cattle Company had been incorporated, with President B.P. Morse, Secretary J.P.M. Humphrey, and principal stockholder A.E. Reynolds as signers. The transaction was not legalized until five years after Reynolds' death in March 1921.[3]

Legal donor or not, at this same meeting in November 1920, A.E. Reynolds then regaled the group with his recollections of

[2] La Junta Chapter, DAR.

[3] Fragmented press clipping; fragmented copy of the Articles of Incorporation, notarized before Elizabeth Smith, N.P., City and County of Denver, La Junta Chapter, DAR. The Bent's Fort Land and Cattle Company was a Reynolds family affair. The donor in 1926 was Reynolds's only surviving heir, his daughter Anna (Louisa W. Arps to Merrill J. Mattes, 23 May 1978).

the fort from the time of his first visit there in 1867. Concerning this meeting, the local newspaper identified the guests of honor as A.E. Reynolds of Denver and Frank Mixon of La Junta (rather than Williams), Mixon being another knowledgable old-timer. According to this account also, "the ladies are enthusiastic in their endeavours to reconstruct the historic old building and make it the chief attraction of this territory." At the same time Mrs. J.E. Rice, regent of the La Junta Chapter, announced that Edward H. Ayers of Chicago "had become interested in the work and offered a gift of $250 toward the reconstruction of the old landmark."[4] So resurrection or re-creation of the fabled adobe castle was definitely on the agenda fifty-six years before the miracle finally came to pass.

On 21 April 1921 a community picnic and tree-planting festival was sponsored by the La Junta Chapter, a notable occasion reported in the local press:

> A large delegation of La Junta citizens went to the site of old Fort Bent Tuesday for the purpose of setting out trees around the site, and along the road leading from the Santa Fe Trail to the place . . . .
> . . . The trees — elm and ash — were all goodsized specimens, and were in good condition for replanting. Two hundred were planted on this day.
> George Williams, foreman of the Reynolds ranch, had provided teams and plows, and . . . the entire east line of the road leading to the fort was set with trees, the driveway around the site was lined on both sides with trees, and a small park was made in one corner . . . .
> The first tree planted . . . was set out by Mrs. J.E. Rice . . . who first conceived the idea of rebuilding the old ruins, and of beautifying the grounds by planting some hardy varieties of trees.
> A fence will be built in the near future, and the re-building of the walls will follow later. A number of men in different parts of the country are interested in the project and have promised financial assistance.[5]

At the May 1921 meeting the treasurer presented bills of $50.00 for trees, $33.00 for posts, $13.60 for hauling posts, and $55.20 for wire. It was then voted that a sign board be placed at the entrance "until the archway should be completed." The cemented cobblestone gateway arch, which is still in existence,

[4] La Junta Chapter, DAR, including unidentified press clipping, dated 16 November 1920. For A.E. Reynolds reminiscences, *see* article by Louisa Arps in this issue of *The Colorado Magazine*. Edward H. Ayers later became the donor of a notable western American history collection to the Newberry Library, Chicago.

[5] Unidentified press clipping with "April 1921" in script, La Junta Chapter, DAR.

This early 1960s view of the fort site, looking through the cobblestone gateway arch, shows the Santa Fe marker (left) and the Baldridge equipment shed (right).

was not actually erected until several years later, at a cost of $391.32, "to which schoolchildren, among others, contributed." The designer of this arch was George Hine, a La Junta city engineer. The dedication services, with Judge M.F. Miller giving the principal address, took place "about July 1930."[6]

Despite setbacks and disappointments, such as a 1925 report that one-half of the trees planted in 1921 had died, there were other efforts to improve the premises. At an October 1924 meeting the members voted to "put on a play after Christmas for the benefit of the same." In 1925 the La Junta City Council offered the services of the city surveyor to survey the boundaries. In 1929 the rough-graded access road was declared to be a county road by the commissioners. There may have been other fundraising efforts, but during the Depression, through World War II, and for eight years thereafter, it must be said that the restoration project languished, even as the ancient adobe mounds on the Arkansas River continued their inexorable process of disintegration.[7]

While the historic importance of Bent's Old Fort was never in doubt, the site itself, identifiable only as a rough spot on a rather undistinguished landscape, was not a very exciting proposition to any but the most dedicated patriots and history stu-

---

[6] La Junta Chapter, DAR; item in "Golden Anniversary Program," 9 November 1963, held near the fort site at the home of the first park superintendent, La Junta Chapter, DAR.

[7] La Junta Chapter, DAR; as for DAR picnics, in 1953 Mrs. J.E. Rice stated: "In 1922 we had another clean-up day and picnic, but I am sorry to say we have never had another one" (*La Junta Tribune-Democrat,* 21 February 1953).

dents. The DAR Chapter, to its eternal credit, performed the crucial service of preserving the site from extinction and providing monumentation, and there was brave talk of rebuilding, but anything resembling actual restoration under the La Junta DAR auspices, with its slender resources, was wishful thinking. It probably occurred to more than one imaginative citizen of the community that another owner might achieve something more tangible. Why not the State of Colorado with its considerable resources and its pride in its frontier heritage?

It appears that a La Junta citizens group took the first step in this direction. In August 1952 Harry C. Reese of the La Junta Chamber of Commerce, George Cosand of the Otero County Historical Society, and G.E. Kimball, state representative, requested an audience with Dr. LeRoy R. Hafen, executive director of the State Historical Society of Colorado, "to talk about Bent's Fort restoration possibilities." The meeting took place in Dr. Hafen's office in early December 1952. Among those present (in addition to the above) were James Grafton Rogers, president of the Society, and Mrs. D.R. Lee, representing Mrs. Warder Lee Braerton, state regent of the DAR. The Society officials agreed that the fort should be restored as "an official Colorado historical site" and promised an investigation.[8]

The idea that the State Historical Society of Colorado should assume responsibility for the area evidently caught fire rapidly, for the 1953 Colorado General Assembly, through Senate Bill 84, declared Bent's Old Fort on the Arkansas River to be one of five historic sites in a new category of State Historical Monuments under the management and control of the Society (as, if and when acquired, if not already owned). This act, shepherded through the legislature by Society Secretary Stephen H. Hart, also authorized the Society to "restore, repair, construct, install, and furnish, in its discretion, and to the extent of moneys available to it, such buildings, museums and other structures and such exhibits, and displays as seemed advisable." The La Junta DAR evidently went along cheerfully with the idea of a more ambitious preservation project, for on 14 June 1954 the deed conveying "for the consideration of one dollar" 4.41 acres of land "to the State of Colorado for the use and benefit of the State Historical Society" was signed by Mabel G. Robinson, regent,

[8] Harry C. Reese to LeRoy R. Hafen, 4 August 1952, Bent's Old Fort Correspondence files, State Historical Society of Colorado (hereinafter referred to as CF-SHSC); *La Junta Tribune-Democrat*, 15 December 1952. Dr. Hafen disclaims any role in the fort takeover (Hafen, Palm Desert, California, to Merrill J. Mattes, 6 November 1975).

and Clara Bell Humphries, secretary, the La Junta Chapter, Daughters of the American Revolution.[9]

Although its financial resources at this time were evidently meager, the Society Board of Directors, under the vigorous leadership of James Grafton Rogers, promptly took two steps toward the goal of a more meaningful historic site. The first step was to set up a Bent's Fort Restoration Advisory Committee. Original nominees were Mrs. L.P. Strain of La Junta, representing the DAR Chapter, Henry Frank, Jr., a Bent's Old Fort neighbor, George Cosand, of the Otero County Historical Society, and Chester E. Beck and Inez Nelson of Las Animas. A belated, but inspired, appointment was that of Dr. John K. Johnston, D.V.M., of La Junta, then owner of the lands surrounding the site. Beck thanked Rogers for "the privilege to be associated with so noble and glorious a work."[10] The idea, perhaps, was glorious but there would be no noble work for two more decades. There is no evidence that this short-lived committee ever served in other than an honorary capacity but, representing a cross-section of local support, it did give visibility to the Society's somewhat nebulous presence.

The second and the more significant step taken by the Society was to arrange for an archaeological investigation of the site by Professor Herbert W. Dick of Trinidad State Junior College. This research began under the aegis of Society President Rogers, with field work coordinated by Deputy Curator James T. Forrest. In October 1953 Governor Daniel Thornton was asked to approve the expenditure of $500.00 "for preliminary work at the site" so that "restoration will begin soon, in a small way."[11] On 18 May 1954 a Memorandum of Agreement between the Society and the junior college was co-signed by Agnes Wright Spring, executive assistant to Rogers, and Dwight Baird, president of the junior college. This provided for an estimated forty-two days of excavation work at the site in the summer of 1954, with $569.80 in cash to be provided by the Society, and an estimated cash equivalent value of $3,150 in professional services, labor, and equipment to be supplied by the college. Of special interest is the language of the agreement, setting forth the objective of the Society:

[9] James Grafton Rogers, "President's Annual Report," *The Colorado Magazine* 31 (January 1954):1-2; copy of deed in CF-SHSC. The irregular tract of land on the old Santa Fe Trail, consisting of the fort site itself and a strip of land 40 feet wide from the site to the public road, is described as "a part of the SW¼ of Sec. 14 and of the NW¼ of Sec. 23, Twp 23 S., Rg. 54 W."

[10] James Grafton Rogers to each of indicated nominees, 8, 9 October 1953, Rogers to John K. Johnston, 21 January 1954, Chester E. Beck to Rogers, 1 July 1954, CF-SHSC.

[11] Agnes Wright Spring to Daniel Thornton, 21 October 1953, CF-SHSC.

Whereas the Society plans to reconstruct the Fort as an historic museum for public education, but as the fort was constructed chiefly of adobe and has through a century of disuse melted almost to ground level, the Society finds it necessary to have the area excavated under the direction of skilled experts and scholars, to determine its outlines and construction, mark its area for public view, recover what relics may be buried in the ruins, and prepare it for future development.[12]

Had Bent's Old Fort ever been excavated before? A newspaper article of November 1953 stated what was presumably common knowledge: "During the years many interested persons have dug around the foundations, possibly destroying valuable historical data." This much is hearsay but most other evidence is circumstantial — the presence of "artifacts from Bent's Old Fort" in various private collections. There is, however, at least one document from another excavation. In February 1952 a well-meaning La Junta citizen wrote Dr. Hafen to advise him of a free-lance amateur project:

We believe we are going to locate the walls of the Fort quite accurately. We have found traces of adobe bricks of both the west and north wall, and of the tower on the northwest corner. We recovered a quantity of ox shoes, mule shoes, tools, clay pipe stem, etc. last Saturday. The material is mounted and a record is being made of the location. We think we hit the blacksmith shop . . . . We lifted the artifacts carefully, leaving the rust encrustations intact . . . . Would you advise as to the best technique for care?[13]

The first scientific excavation of the fort took place in early November 1953 when, presumably at the behest of Forrest, Trinidad archaeologist Dick spent three days digging at the site to establish the northwest corner and to ascertain the thickness of the walls of the main fort — twenty seven inches. This first effort attracted carloads of state and local dignitaries to witness the historic occasion. A newspaper headline exuberantly reported progress, "Search Pinpoints Fort Bent Corner." The accompanying article quoted old-timers who remembered when the crumbling walls were high enough to shelter cattle.[14]

---

[12] Memorandum of Agreement, CF-SHSC.

[13] *Pueblo Chieftain*, 21 November 1953. "Time and hundreds of curiosity seekers . . . ravaged the site years before [archaeologists] moved in to search for items of significance" (*Lamar Tri-State Daily News*, 18 March 1966); C.T. Pringle, La Junta, to Hafen, 11 February 1952, CF-SHSC. Aside from the fact that such projects violate laws against digging on private or public lands, professional archaeologists object because they simply destroy valuable and irreplaceable evidence.

[14] *La Junta Tribune-Democrat*, 3 November 1953.

Excavating a channel in the northwest tower in 1954.

Utilizing student labor the main official excavation took place from 20 June to 23 July 1954 under Herbert Dick's supervision, with his wife Martha Dick as a camp cook, under much-publicized primitive conditions and with temperatures as high as 106 degrees Farenheit. The enterprise attracted dozens of eager "sidewalk superintendents," and caused further newspaper fanfare, yielding headlines such as "Expectancy Hovers over Bent Diggings."[15]

Shortly after the dig, when dreams of quick restoration were in full flower, some currency was given to a suggestion that the less valuable "scrap" in the collection be sold to the public to raise money for such a restoration. Professor Dick was properly horrified at the idea, and wrote Forrest: "If I were you I would not throw a single item away! Do not sell any of it. Keep the entire collection intact."[16] Fortunately, this misguided idea was strangled in infancy.

[15] *Arkansas Valley Journal,* 17 June 1954; *La Junta Tribune-Democrat,* 6 July, 2 August, 1954; *Denver Rocky Mountain News,* 11 June 1954, *Denver Post, Empire Magazine,* n.d.

    Professor Dick's report to the Society was delayed until February 1956 because of his academic and other research commitments. Details are omitted here since this report was subsequently published in *The Colorado Magazine.* Artifacts recovered from this excavation, though later available for examination and analysis by NPS investigators, now repose in the collections of the Society and will remain there as a matter of policy. Some artifacts from the dig have been retained at the Trinidad College Museum, presumably on an indefinite loan basis since the Memorandum of Agreement stipulated that "all results, findings and materials shall belong to the Society" (Herbert W. Dick, "The Excavation of Bent's Old Fort, Otero County, Colorado," *The Colorado Magazine* 33 [July 1956]:181-96; W.E. Marshall, SHSC, to Nan Carson, NPS, Omaha, 31 August 1965, CF-SHSC; interview with Dr. Wilfred D. Logan, 16 October 1975, Denver Service Center, NPS [hereinafter cited as DSC-NPS]; Jackson W. Moore, Jr., to Research Archaeologist, Midwest Rgional Office, 20 August 1965; "Progress Reports on Bent's Old Fort," DSC-NPS).

[16] Herbert W. Dick to James T. Forrest, 27 February 1955, CF-SHSC.

With this somewhat exciting research project out of the way, the Society was confronted with the stark problem of what to do next. There was copious talk of restoration by Society officials as well as Arkansas River valley citizens, but there was no money for such a purpose, and obviously, there was no real awareness of the wide chasm between the cost of a bona fide restoration and the depressed condition of finances, both state and local. However, what must be kept in mind about this period of Society custodianship is that, despite the meagerness of results following lofty intentions, the dream of restoration was kept vigorously alive.

Early in 1953 in a lecture at Rocky Ford, Edgar C. Mc-Mechen, then curator of the Colorado State Museum, had proclaimed that "Bent's Fort is without doubt the most important site in Colorado." He predicted that "rebuilding and equipping the fort may be one of the largest projects approved by the State Historical Society." He also came up with the novel suggestion that "in restoring the fort some provision should be made for tourists who wish to sleep at the fort."[17] Although not so stated, it seems probable that what McMechen had in mind was the adaptation of the fort to a unique kind of motel, which would help defray the cost of restoration and upkeep.

In his "Annual Report of the President" for 1954, Rogers restated the Society's position on Bent's Old Fort: "The Society took over on the understanding that as means permitted we would reconstruct the old mud castle and open it as a museum . . . . There is great interest in Bent and Otero Counties in the project and with their help we hope to make progress, first in completing acquisition of the ground we need and then in gradual reconstruction."[18]

Though the Society's official position was, thus, hedged with caution, the 1954 dig somehow created an impression in the Arkansas River valley community that substantial restoration could somehow be achieved in fairly short order. By 1955, however, the euphoria had been dissipated and a sense of reality began to pervade the correspondence. Early in 1955 the La Junta Chamber of Commerce secretary, while assuring the Society that local leaders "are enthusiastic" about "ideas that have been developed," raised a novel question. He wrote that "I am

[17] *La Junta Tribune-Democrat*, 6, 7 June 1953.
[18] James Grafton Rogers, "President's Annual Report," *The Colorado Magazine* 32 (January 1955): 9-10.

beginning to wonder if there isn't some merit to a program of preserving the ruins exactly as they are and not try to reconstruct any part of those existing. Rather than counterfeiting construction in this sense, why not build to one side with permanent material — one tower and a modern building for display of items and dioramas?" Curator Forrest expressed little enthusiasm for this more modest goal: "I think there is merit in the idea if preservation of what little remains, such as they are, can be preserved without actually destroying the appearance of same. If the appearance must be changed, then it seems that we have not accomplished anything other than outlining the Fort itself."[19]

While the restoration idea hovered in the background, there were a few unglamorous things that could actually be accomplished. A National Park Service ruins stabilization specialist from Chaco Canyon was consulted about the ways and the means of preserving the exposed fort's remains. The Society designed a "desk-like information stand" for placement at the site. There was a project to have Herbert Dick resurvey the fort's walls and define these with the placement of painted stakes for the benefit of the visiting public. The scale of the operations in 1955 may be gleaned from the fact that the budget for the fort totaled $200.00, of which $111.00 was set aside for the staking project, $50.00 "for improving park" in unspecified ways, and $10.00 for "installation of orientation marker." George Cosand of La Junta then handled the Society business locally on a volunteer basis, while Maurice Frink, the new executive director of the Society, assumed a role in the Bent's Old Fort affairs.[20]

In February 1956 Rogers and Frink attended a meeting of the Colorado Arkansas Valley (CAVI) at Pueblo. Max L.A. Sauder of La Junta, president of this promotional organization, expressed an interest in helping the worthy cause along. The upshot was a new CAVI Bent's Fort Committee, appointed by Sauder, with a membership including Mmes. James Taylor, J.E. Rice, and Bert Oldham representing the La Junta DAR, Dr. Johnston, George Cosand, and Carroll Wright representing the La Junta Chamber of Commerce, and Marticia Thomas of Swink, CAVI secretary.[21]

---

[19] Reese to Forrest, 2 February 1955, Forrest to Reese, 21 February 1955, CF-SHSC.

[20] Reese to Gordon C. Vivian, Chaco Canyon National Monument, New Mexico, NPS, 16 February 1955; Forrest to George Cosand, 8 April 1955; Maurice Frink to Cosand, 27 June 1955, CF-SHSC.

[21] Frink, typed notes on meeting, 23 February 1955, CF-SHSC.

In July Rogers and Frink visited La Junta to meet with the committee, now chaired by Dr. Johnston, "owner of the ranch which surrounds Bent's Fort." Rogers announced that "the Society is ready to make headway on the project, can put one thousand to several thousand a year into it, and wishes to proceed at once," but under certain salient conditions:

1. that the fort corral area of about one acre be added to the Society's holdings as a donation;

2. that an additional ten acres, "so laid out as to facilitate future development of the area," be acquired locally from Dr. Johnston and then deeded to the state since "the Society has no funds to buy land";

3. that an overall long-term plan for development be prepared, "so that every step taken will be in conformity with the ultimate design";

4. that the plan include reconstruction of some part of the original fort, perhaps the northeast watch tower and part of the wall, "this to be done with adobe brick as nearly as possible like those in the original fort";

5. that a plan be devised for improving access, "so that it would not be necessary to pass through Dr. Johnston's barnyard";

6. that liaison with the Society be maintained through a chairman with the time and the ability to serve as local manager of the project (without pay) "and would see that matters did not lag."[22]

At the meeting it was agreed that the city engineer of La Junta was competent "to put the plan on paper," presumably on a volunteer basis. As it turned out this official was preoccupied with plans for a new city building and no such plans ever materialized, at least in tangible form for the record. The Society was more fortunate in its choice of a local, unpaid manager. Dr. Johnston accepted this responsibility and did proceed with a few constructive steps, plans or no plans. These included painting signs, repairing gates, and spreading five tons of salt over the fort site to discourage weeds. However, plans to have the dead trees removed by the county were thwarted because the county commissioner involved was busy campaigning for reelection. As to the additional land needed, Dr. Johnston indicated that his land could be obtained but "not until I know that

22 Ibid, 20 July 1955, CF-SHSC.

something concrete was being done on the restoration of the Fort."[23]

Early in 1957 Dr. Johnston sold his property to James Baldridge who thereafter would figure prominently in the affairs of the fort. In February and March meetings with the new landowner Milt Andrus of the La Junta Chamber of Commerce, and others, Rogers and Frink laid out a program that was, in large degree, contingent on Baldridge's donation of the additional land, principally the old corral area. Three things helped to influence the landowner favorably. First, to demonstrate serious intentions of the Society, Herbert Dick was persuaded to come over from Trinidad to run some trenches to verify the location of the corral wall and to stake twelve reference points outlining the complete fort. Second, a resurvey of the state property was conducted to verify the accuracy of the 1954 survey and to establish boundaries for the proposed addition. Third, Baldridge was hired as a "local supervisor" at the rate of "one dollar an hour with maximum of one hundred dollars in any one calendar month." The gratifying result, on 22 April, was the assignment of a deed to the state by James H. Baldridge and wife for 0.667 of an acre.[24]

This small, but significant, addition triggered several improvements. By the end of June the Society had expended over $3,000 on a water well and pump, pit toilet, grass seed, mower, and a contract with the Southeast Colorado Power Association. Local volunteers coordinated by Andrus helped with the construction of picnic facilities, and Al Miller, a county commissioner, staked out and arranged to have the approach road and the parking area graded.[25]

The most imaginative development in 1957 was a symbolic start on the restoration by outlining the fort walls with new adobe brick. In October Frink reported that:

> We have constructed several thousand adobe brick [and] have laid some of them up in a rough outline of the old fort. We are not attempting a permanent reconstruction . . . .

[23] Johnston to Frink, 31 August, 23 April, 9 May, 27 October 1956, CF-SHSC.

[24] Frink, typed notes on meetings, 26-27 February, 28 March 1957; Dick to Frink, 30 March 1957. (There is no evidence that the earlier staking project was ever carried out.) Frink to Milt Andrus, La Junta, 7 March 1957 (the original survey of T 23 S, R 54 W, Sixth Principal Meridian, was performed in 1869 and 1882 by "Deputy Surveyor Geo. Hill" [Lowell M. Puckett, Bureau of Land Management, to superintendent, 20 January 1964, files, State Office, Bureau of Land Management, Denver]); Frink to James Baldridge, 4 April 1957; copy of deed, CF-SHSC.

[25] Andrus to Frink, 12 April 1957; Frink, "Notes on Expenditures," 28 May 1957, CF-SHSC.

> What we are trying to do is, with the expenditure of a thousand dollars or so from our meagre budget plus another thousand or so that the La Junta community is trying to raise, indicate on the ground the floor plan of the fort so that visitors may visualize what the old adobe castle was like in a general way. We have already built the north wall up to a height of about five feet straight across. The other outer walls we plan to keep only two or three feet high, with an irregular top. The room arrangements may be indicated by a single row of brick laid on the ground.
>
> The bricks we are using for this purpose were made of mud taken from the ground a hundred feet from the fort site. They are the size of the original brick, 14 × 8 × 4", ... Cut straw was mixed with the mud. No asphalt or other preparation was used.[26]

The effort in 1957 appears to have been the extent of the state restoration because sizeable contributions promised locally simply did not materialize. In March Andrus told Frink that the local historical society "pledged $250 and promised to go out and raise more." However, as of 22 July 1957, Frink indicated that no outside donations had actually been forthcoming and state funds were nearly exhausted, since the bricks were costing twenty cents each, more than double what was anticipated. He urged that local fund-raising efforts be renewed. If successful, "we could then have a big public gathering at the Fort site in the early autumn." In reply Andrus expressed confidence that $1,500.00 or more could be raised "within thirty days." The hollowness of this prediction is evident from a report of 9 December from Marticia Thomas, CAVI treasurer, that the sum total contributed from all sources up to that time was $265.00, of which CAVI was credited for $100.00 and the Otero County Society for $50.00. There is no record of further donations locally, except for $426.50 from the La Junta Chamber of Commerce.[27]

The token adobe construction in 1957 described by Frink seems to have been the high water mark of the involvement of the State of Colorado. In 1958-59 there was talk of further plans and more fund-raising, but at this juncture efforts at the state and the local levels really began to concentrate on a philosophy of turning the whole problem over to the United States government — if that source of so many other blessings could be

---

[26] Frink to Vivian, 14 October 1957, CF-SHSC.

[27] Andrus to Frink, 3 March 1957; Frink to Max L.A. Sauder, La Junta, 22 July 1957; Frink to Baldridge, 14 October 1957; Marticia Thomas to Frink, 9 December 1957; Baldridge to Frink, 18 February 1959, CF-SHSC.

persuaded to accept the honor. It was in fact in April 1956 that the thought first appears in Society correspondence, when Dr. Johnston suggested that Frink accompany him to Las Vegas, New Mexico, "to find out how they got the National Monument idea across at Fort Union." In May of that same year he reported that "our Chamber of Commerce Secretary recently returned from a national meeting where he met the assistant in the National Monument Service and he was informed that Bent's Fort was on the list to be inspected as a possible National Monument." This was probably the consequence of a letter from Frink to Senator Gordon Allott "asking what steps might be taken to make Bent's Fort a National Monument." The senator referred the inquiry to the Department of the Interior in early April 1956. Although the Society had received no overt encouragement along these lines as of October 1957, Frink confided to Baldridge, who served as foreman on the adobe project, that "we have reason to think that the federal government may at some future time, take over the Bent's Fort site. When and if this happens, doubtless a thorough-going and costly job of reconstruction will be done. This is a hope for the long-range future, and convinces us that our part now should be to provide for the short-range future. Therefore the outlining of the rest of the wall should be done on an admittedly temporary basis."[28]

In December 1957 Rogers asked Senator John A. Carroll to approach the National Park Service (NPS) about taking over both Bent's Old Fort in Otero County and Pikes Stockade in Conejos County. He explained: "The motive of the Society is simply to lighten our responsibility by having the national government take over two tracts which are suitable and dignified for its historic program and by doing so release our always limited Society resources to care for a number of other museums of more local historical character." In February 1958 Acting Director Eivind Scoyen of the NPS in Washington, D.C., advised Senator Carroll:

> In conducting the National Survey of Historic Sites and Buildings that the National Park Service resumed this year [after interruption by World War II] we plan to give priority to the theme of Western Expansion, and instructions to that effect have been given to the field personnel conducting the site work. Both Bent's Fort and Pike's Stockade fall in this theme. Accordingly, it is our intent and present hope that

[28] Johnston to Frink, 23 April, 9 May 1956; Frink to Johnston, 1 May 1956; Frink to Baldridge, 14 October 1957, CF-SHSC.

investigations, at least preliminary, on both these sites can be accomplished this year . . . .

As soon as the Survey is completed . . . and a critical evaluation of it made by the Advisory Board on Historic Sites, Buildings, and Monuments, we will be in a better position than now to advise what place these historic landmarks should have in the National Park System, or whether they might more appropriately be the responsibility of another agency.[29]

Historians at the Omaha office of the NPS under the direction of Merrill Mattes, regional chief of history and archaeology, were assigned to research Bent's Old Fort and to submit a report to document the factor of national significance. With the wealth of historical data available, they had no problem in recognizing the historical merits of the old trading post, despite the fact that ninety-nine percent of the original structure had disappeared.[30] Accordingly, the region's favorable recommendation breezed through channels, and the National Park Service Advisory Board at its April 1959 meeting concurred, identifying the fort as one of five sites associated with the Santa Fe Trail to be "classified as having exceptional value in illustrating and commemorating this important part of our national heritage."[31] Thus encouraged, Senator Allott promptly drafted S. 1833, "authorizing the establishment of a National Historic Site at Bent's Old Fort near La Junta, Colorado." He implored Senator Clinton Anderson, acting chairman of the Senate Subcommittee on Public Lands that "if there is any chance that the Subcommittee could act on this bill this year, it would be greatly appreciated," inasmuch as such establishment "has been favorably recommended by the National Park Service Advisory Board." At this point the senator was one jump ahead of the NPS, since the "exceptional value" label was not actually the equivalent of an endorsement for federal ownership. Nevertheless, when on 11 May the Department of the Interior asked the NPS for its views on S. 1833, Acting Director Scoyen advised that "the National

29 Rogers to John A. Carroll, 18 December 1957; Eivind Scoyen to Carroll, 3 February 1958, CF-SHSC.

30 Ray H. Mattison, unpublished report, Washington, D.C., Office, NPS (hereinafter cited as WASO-NPS).

31 Fred A. Seaton, secretary of the interior, Washington, D.C., to Senator Gordon Allott, 16 April 1959, files, WASO-NPS. The four other sites are Fort Larned and Wagon Bed Springs, Kansas, Raton Pass in Colorado and New Mexico, and the historic district, Santa Fe, New Mexico.

Park Service recommends that the Department interpose no objection to the enactment of this legislation."[32]

The subcommittee was not in a hurry, however, and the hearings were postponed until the NPS could answer some hard questions. It now developed that something more than the "national significance" label was needed, namely a "suitability and feasibility study." In 1959 the National Park System consisted of about two hundred areas, funding was a chronic problem, and any proposal to add yet another area to its collection, with its perpetual obligations, was not to be taken lightly. While sympathetic to Colorado's proposal, the NPS had to undertake further study before it could be defended conscientiously before the subcommittee. On 14 May Scoyen confided to the regional director in Omaha that "we believe that the Fort merits consideration for status as a unit of the System," but he instructed the region to schedule a detailed investigation of the area, particularly boundary requirements for a viable unit, land ownership, and cost data.[33]

David L. Hieb, regional chief of boundary studies, was designated the team leader on the feasibility and boundary study, which was completed in October. This brief document unequivocally recommended the establishment of a National Historic Site on grounds not only of national significance but also that the site itself had a high degree of integrity inasmuch as the archaeological remains were certifiably authentic, and the environs of the site, comprising farmland and river bottom, would not clash visually with objectives of preservation and possible reconstruction. The report also identified the site as a feasible addition to the National Park System because of good accessibility. The site was only seven miles from La Junta and readily accessible from U.S. Highway 50. Finally, it was recognized that the five acres in state ownership would hardly be sufficient space to protect the setting and ensure proper development, so a future boundary encompassing approximately one hundred seventy acres was suggested. The rationale for this boundary reads in part:

> This area consists of about 48 acres of brush grown river flood plain or sandbars, an equal amount of fair low level pasture land, 54 acres of irrigable land, the J.H. Baldridge

[32] Allott to Clinton Anderson, 20 July 1959; Scoyen to legislative counsel, Office of the Solicitor, Department of the Interior, 3 June 1959, WASO-NPS.

[33] Scoyen to regional director, Region Two, 14 May 1959, WASO-NPS.

farmstead and the small area owned by the State of Colorado. . . .
This is considered to be the minimum area adequate to provide a reasonable setting in which to interpret the fort site and to provide for a proper approach road, parking area, and essential employee quarters and utility structures reasonably well separated from the historic site. It includes subsidiary historic sites such as that of one of the historic river crossings, an icehouse located on the river bank southwest of the fort site, and part of the level area northwest of the fort reputedly used extensively for trader and Indian horse races. It utilizes the natural boundary of the river on two sides and the practical boundary of the State Highway on the third, while on the west straight lines closely paralleling a natural division of the irrigable land were selected to permit easy adjustment of the field laterals affected. Any reduction of the area would perpetuate the existing threat of intrusions too close to the fort site and eliminate the possibility of restoring a small area of the fort site's surroundings to a likeness of its historic condition.[34]

After wending its way through bureaucratic channels in Omaha and Washington, D.C., the feasibility and boundary study reached the desk of Fred A. Seaton, secretary of the interior, who was then in a position to assure congressional subcommittees that Bent's Old Fort was indeed worthy of their endorsement. As the result of the diligence of Senator Allott and Congressman J. Edgar Chenoweth of the Colorado Third District, twin bills "establishing a National Historic Site at Bent's Old Fort near La Junta, Colorado" had been reframed and were under consideration in both houses of Congress, namely S. 1833, by the Committee on Interior and Insular Affairs in the Senate and H.R. 6851 by the committee of the same name in the House of Representatives.[35] On 21 December 1959 Assistant Secretary Roger Ernst wrote identical letters to Chairman James E. Murray of the Senate committee and Chairman Wayne N. Aspinall of the House committee:

> Your committee has requested a report on S. 1833 . . . .
> We recommend the enactment of this legislation . . . .
> The site would be administered by the National Park Service under the direction of the Secretary of the Interior, and the Secretary would be authorized to construct and maintain such markers, buildings, and other improvements on the site to take care of visitors as he might deem necessary.

---

[34] Unpublished report, WASO-NPS; Howard W. Baker, regional director, Omaha, to Frink, 4 April 1960, CF-SHSC.

[35] Copies of Senate Report 1224 and House of Representatives Report 1393, 86th Cong., 2d sess., CF-SHSC, and in files, Bent's Old Fort National Historic Site (hereinafter referred to as BOFS-NPS).

The Advisory Board on National Parks, Historic Sites, Buildings and Monuments has recently classified Bent's Old Fort as having exceptional value in commemorating and illustrating the history of the United States. In considering the sites associated with the Santa Fe Trail we are of the opinion that of the five sites classified by the Advisory Board, Bent's Old Fort would be one of the prime choices for rounding out the National Park System.

Bent's Old Fort was one of the great centers of the fur trade during the height of its activity in the Rocky Mountains. It played a unique, interesting and enduring part in the development of the pioneer settlement of the Southwest, flourishing in a heroic age, with a history steeped in romance . . . .

The Bureau of the Budget has advised us that there is no objection to the submission of this report to your committee.

The assistant secretary recommended an amendment to the original bill, the effect of which would be to authorize the acquisition of less than fee simple title. "This is highly desirable in order to provide sufficient flexibility to enable us to acquire lands subject to continued use and occupancy, when administratively desirable."[36]

On 24 February supplemental data regarding the historical authenticity of the area and cost estimates for land acquisition were submitted by the director to the subcommittees, at their request. On 15 March the House committee submitted the bill to "the Committee of the Whole House on the State of the Union," reporting favorable action by the committee, with the suggested amendment. The committee report respected the sentiment that the site of the fort would be a valuable addition to the National Park System and anticipated the need for "about 170 acres of land," also that the estimated land acquisition cost would be $46,240. Of the 170 acres to be acquired, about 5 were owned by the State of Colorado. This, it was understood, would be made available to the government without cost. On 1 April 1960 a similar favorable report was made to the Senate by Gordon Allott of that committee.[37]

The Senate bill was passed without objection. The House bill ran into a small snag in the form of Representative H.E. Gross of Iowa who protested in this vein:

The reason I am so strongly opposed is the fact that for all time the taxpayers of the Nation will be called upon to maintain and manage this site.

---

[36] BOFS-NPS.

[37] Scoyen to regional director, Region Two, 7 March 1960, WASO-NPS; BOFS-NPS.

If, as contended by the proponents, this site should be
maintained why should not the expense be borne by the State
of Colorado? Why unload it upon all the taxpayers at a time
when Congress is preparing to again boost the Federal debt
which now stands at some $290 billion?
Mr. Speaker, I should like to add that I am surprised that
the Department of the Interior, which is part of an administration that professes to be interested in economy and "belt tight-
ening," supports this bill and many others of a similar nature
which call for the spending of funds for projects which could be
delayed until the finances of this Nation are put in order.[38]

Despite the lone watchdog role of Gross, the bill was passed
by the House on 25 May 1960 and then re-passed in the form of
S. 1833. When the bill was signed by President Dwight D.
Eisenhower on 3 June 1960, it became Public Law 86-487 of the
86th Congress, "Authorizing the establishment of a national
historic site at Bent's Old Fort near La Junta, Colorado."

Be it enacted by the Senate and House of Representatives
of the United States of America in Congress assembled, That
the Secretary of the Interior shall acquire on behalf of the
United States, by gift, purchase, condemnation, or otherwise,
such lands, interests therein and improvements thereon, as
the Secretary may deem necessary for the purpose of establishing a national historic site at the site of Bent's Old Fort on
the Old Santa Fe Trail, located in Otero County, Colorado,
approximately seven miles east of La Junta, north of the
Arkansas River.
SEC. 2. (a) The property acquired under the provisions of
the first section of this Act shall be designated as the Bent's
Old Fort National Historic Site and shall be set aside as a
public national memorial to commemorate the historic role
played by such fort in the opening of the West. The National
Park Service, under the direction of the Secretary of the Interior, shall administer, protect, and develop such monument,
subject to the provisions of the Act entitled "An Act to establish a National Park Service, and for other purposes," approved August 25, 1916, as amended and supplemented, and
the Act entitled "An Act to provide for the preservation of
historic American sites, buildings, objects, and antiquities of
national significance, and for other purposes," approved August 21, 1935, as amended.
(b) In order to provide for the proper development and
maintenance of such national historic site, the Secretary of the
Interior is authorized to construct and maintain therein such
markers, buildings, and other improvements, and such
facilities for the care and accommodation of visitors, as he may
deem necessary.

---

[38] *Congressional Digest*, 25 May 1960.

SEC. 3. There are hereby authorized to be appropriated such sums as may be necessary to carry out the provisions of this Act.[39]

Passage of the act did not automatically result in the NPS moving in with perfected plans and plenty of money to implement them. In fact there were no funds whatever appropriated initially, and no major development was to occur for fifteen years. Shifting the responsibility from the state to the federal government was a political matter, but adequate funding for plans and improvements was an economic problem for both Congress and the National Park Service with its 200 areas in 1960 swelling to 300 in 1975, and never enough money to do everything for everybody all at once. The rosy expectations that went with this governmental shift were bound to suffer for awhile from the economic realities.

The National Park Service was not delinquent in picking up the ball. Although Colorado did not act with lightning speed in conveying its five acres, the initial problem was the designation of a hypothetical boundary and the lack of funds to acquire adjacent private lands necessary to establish a viable park unit. The Region Two Office in Omaha under Regional Director Howard W. Baker whipped up a storm of correspondence in an effort to solve first things first. Determining a suitable boundary was a relatively simple matter for the Regional Department of Lands. Accordingly, on 29 March 1961 Baker submitted to Director Conrad L. Wirth a drawing for a final boundary for the "Bent's Old Fort National Historic Site Project." A planimeter measurement revealed an actual tract of 178 acres. Baker felt that this complied with the congressional limitation of "around 170 acres," since "a large part of the boundary follows the poorly defined and unstable bank of the Arkansas River and will be subject to annual changes depending on the shifting of the river channel." The desired lands were held in fee by James H. and Martha Baldridge, except for the 5.077 acres held by the State of Colorado. The understandably concerned Baldridge was asked to be patient until land acquisition funds could be found.[40]

---

[39] 74 Stat. 155.

[40] Baker to Conrad L. Wirth, 29 March 1961; George F. Baggley to Baldridge, 26 July 1961, BOFS-NPS.

    It should be noted that files in the superintendent's office at the site supplied most of the documentation regarding NPS activity. Selected items from the Washington, D.C., Office, obtained through the courtesy of Robert M. Utley, assistant director, Office of Historic Preservation, filled in some gaps. The regional files in Denver (formerly in Omaha), which should have

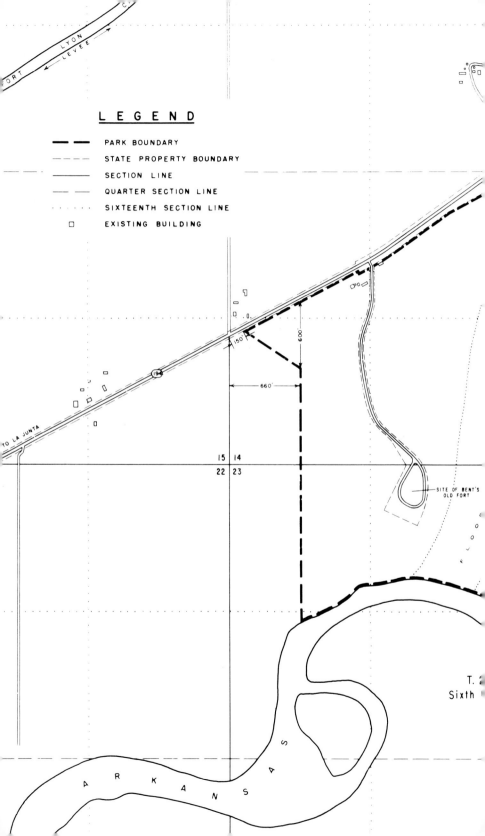

L E G E N D

— — PARK BOUNDARY

— — — STATE PROPERTY BOUNDARY

——— SECTION LINE

— — QUARTER SECTION LINE

· · · · SIXTEENTH SECTION LINE

□ EXISTING BUILDING

LYON
LEVEE
FORT

194

TO LA JUNTA

150'

600'

660'

15 | 14
22 | 23

SITE OF BENT'S
OLD FORT

T. 2
Sixth

A R K A N S A S

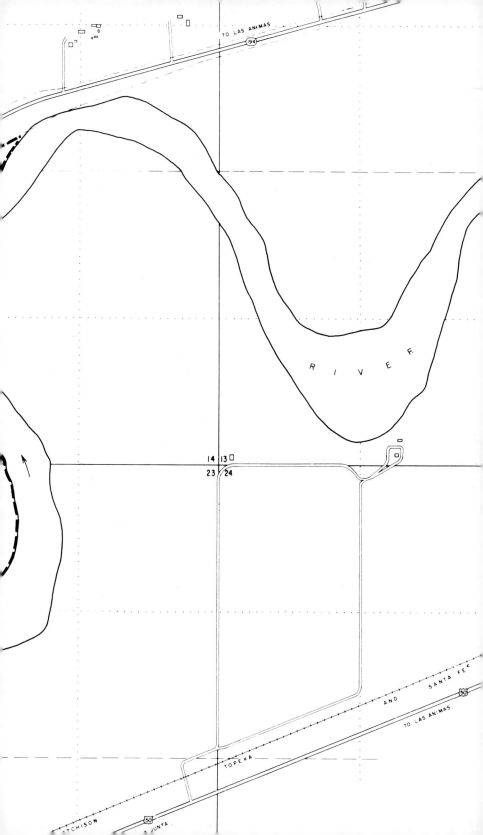

TO LAS ANIMAS

94

R I V E R

14 13
23 24

SANTA FE

AND

TO LAS ANIMAS

50

TOPEKA

ATCHISON

50

A JUNTA

During this period, federal government "economy" was not an empty political slogan. It had teeth in it, so there were no acquisition funds in the treasury for Bent's Old Fort, at least for the moment. Accordingly, the Region Two Office came up with the idea, in which the Society concurred, that perhaps the required acquisition funds could be raised in Colorado (a thought that would have pleased Congressman Gross), possibly among various corporations, such as the Santa Fe or Denver and Rio Grande Western railroads or philanthropic foundations, such as El Pomar, Boettcher, and others. A brochure entitled "Bent's Old Fort National Historic Site Project" dated May 1961 was assembled by David Hieb to indicate boundaries and a development plan, land acquisition cost, and certain curious "advantages of private purchase of land." Copies were sent by Baker to prospective donors, inviting them to help solve the crisis.[41]

In August 1961 when it had become evident that appeals to philanthropy would bear no fruit, Baker dispatched Hieb on the unenviable task of touring Colorado to explore other possibilities with Society Executive Director Frink, various editors, and key personnel of the Arkansas River valley, including officials of Colorado Arkansas Valley (CAVI). After a discouraging two weeks Hieb reported, in effect, that Colorado citizens were all for Bent's Old Fort, but that "none of them had any very clear ideas on how to obtain the necessary funds, either from a few wealthy individuals and organizations or by a widespread publicity campaign."[42] Aside from the question of their economic health in 1961, evidently the Colorado citizenry felt that if they bided their time, the United States government could be depended upon to provide the wherewithal.

On 4 September 1961 Baker reported to Director Wirth that the situation appeared to be hopeless with respect to nonfederal fundraising and urged that "currently appropriated land acquisition funds be used for this purpose." These unearmarked funds were available to the director at his discretion, but they were always woefully inadquate to solve the land acquisition

---

been the main reliance in this sector for the period 1958-73, were mainly missing. It is not clear if these files were lost in transit, or are in dead storage in an unidentified General Services Administration warehouse, or were indiscriminately destroyed in one of the poorly conceived "Records Disposal Programs" promoted by the GSA that have occasionally ravaged old NPS administrative files.

41 Frink to Baker, 20 February; Baggley to Frink, 7 March; Frink to Baggley, 13 March; Baker to Frink, 31 March 1961, CF-SHSC. Baker to Frink, 25 May; Baker to J. Edgar Chenoweth, 24 July 1961, BOFS-NPS. Brochure copies in CF-SHSC and BOFS-NPS.

42 David L. Hieb to Baker, 1 September 1961, BOFS-NPS.

problems of over 200 parks. Nevertheless, it appears that Director Wirth was now persuaded by Senator Gordon Allott to give Bent's Old Fort higher priority at the expense of some other project, for such funds did soon materialize.[43]

Colorado House Bill 234, "Providing for the transfer and conveyance to the United States of America of certain lands in the County of Otero, State of Colorado, now owned by the State for the benefit of the State Historical Society of Colorado," was enacted by the Forty-third Colorado General Assembly and was approved of by Governor Stephen L. McNichols on 13 April 1961. On 31 October the governor executed a deed conveying to the United States of America the 5.077 acres of state land. However, the red tape involved in the abstract of title, possessory rights, mechanic's liens, easements, mineral rights, curative title data, and United States attorney-general review delayed the acceptance of title by the United States until 18 June 1962. In July of that year Baker wrote to Frink about transitional arrangements with the Southeast Colorado Power Association and Baldridge as site custodian.[44] But the National Historic Site still could not become a reality until the private lands also were acquired. This followed at the usual snail-like pace.

The Baldridge property in question was determined by surveyors to comprise 172.923 acres, appraisals were completed, and personnel of the Regional Lands Division proceeded with negotiations. At an undisclosed date in July an agreement was reached with the owners to purchase the property for $41,155.68. Again it was the unavoidable red tape and tax adjustments, not the will of the Region Two Office, that delayed payment to the Baldridges until 26 November and clearance of the title by the Department of Justice until February 1963. In that same month personnel from the Rocky Mountain National Park inspected the area and submitted a required Certificate of Inspection and Possession.[45] Official designation of Bent's Old Fort National Historic Site is filed in the 20 March 1963 issue of the *Federal Register*.

> Notice is hereby given that the following described lands have been acquired on behalf of the United States pursuant to

[43] Baker to Wirth, 4 September 1961, BOFS-NPS; interview with Allott, 6 January 1976.

[44] Frink to Governor Stephen L. McNichols, 27 October 1961, and copy of bill, CF-SHSC; Frink to Baker, 1 November 1961; Baker to Frink, 3 July 1962, BOFS-NPS. This was the original DAR acreage and the parcel donated by Baldridge.

[45] Donald E. Lee, WASO-NPS, to "Accounts," 21 September 1962; Chester C. Brown, Omaha, to James H. and Martha L. Baldridge, 26 November 1962; Allyn F. Hanks to regional director, Omaha, 15 February 1963, BOFS-NPS.

the Act of June 3, 1960 (74 Stat. 155) for establishment of Bent's Old Fort National Historic Site and, effective March 15, 1963, the same are designated as such site:
   All that portion of Indian Claim No. 13 lying within sections 14 and 23, twp. 23 S., rg. 54 W. of the 6th P.M., and bounded as follows: Beginning at a point on the south right-of-way line of Colorado Highway 194, said point being 150 feet northeasterly from the intersection of said south right-of-way line from the west line of section 14; thence northeasterly along said south right-of-way line to its intersection with the Arkansas River; thence southerly and westerly along the Arkansas River through SW¼NE¼, NW¼SE¼, NE¼SW¼, SE¼SW¼, SW¼SE¼, section 14 and through NW¼NE¼, N½NW¼ section 23 to a point in SW¼NW¼ section 23, said point being 660 feet east of the west line of section 23; thence northerly along a line 660 feet east of and parallel to the west lines of sections 23 and 14 to a point 600 feet south of the south right-of-way line of Colorado Highway 194, thence northwesterly to the point of beginning.
   The lands comprising the Bent's Old Fort National Historic Site are hereby set aside as a public national memorial.[46]

At long last the NPS was in business on the Arkansas River — but not yet in a big way. It would be ten more years before funds would become available to make a serious start on the long dreamed of reconstruction. Although currently this seemed to be a period of mere custodianship, with little visible progress, in retrospect it was in fact a period of ferment devoted to three primary activities — the evolution of area management, historical and archaeological research, and planning for the future.

In April 1963 at the request of U.L. Hiatt, president of the Otero County Historical Society, the regional director dispatched Merrill Mattes to La Junta to explain to assembled citizens the new status of the fort and the pending steps by the NPS to make the new park a reality. Foy Young, an experienced park ranger from the Rocky Mountain National Park, was selected as the first superintendent of the area. He arrived in June and occupied the old Baldridge residence, while a trailer was provided as an office facility. Shortly thereafter the new historian position was filled by Dwight E. Stinson, Jr., transferred from Pea Ridge Battlefield in Arkansas. In September Jackson W. Moore, Jr., archaeologist of the Midwest (formerly Region Two) Office arrived to initiate a major project for the comprehensive archaeological excavation of the old fort.

⁴⁶ Copies in CF-SHSC and BOFS-NPS.

Actually, in the absence of planning or development funds, intensive research became the first major activity. The NPS recognized that no intelligent planning could be undertaken until it had a thorough command of the historical and the archaeological data. While there had been spasmodic historical research by the Society and certain individuals, there had never been an all-out effort in this direction. The 1954 archaeological project demonstrated the rough outline of the fort but left most architectural and artifactual questions unanswered. Accordingly, research programs were assigned highest priority. Stinson was assigned full-time to historical research, while Moore was assigned to "the dig." Regional Archaeologist Wilfred Logan supervised the latter project while Merrill Mattes as regional chief of history and archaeology exercised overall research program coordination.

Step number one, of course, after area establishment and securing operational funds to reimburse the new staff, was lining up research money. A program for Stinson involving extensive travel to nationwide research centers required a budget of $5,000, primarily for travel costs, since the historian's salary was already covered. Through the help of Chief Historian Robert Utley in Washington, D.C., this amount was secured for fiscal year 1964 (beginning 1 July 1963).[47] Thus, shortly after his arrival on the scene, Stinson embarked on his project. He had a two-pronged assignment, a "Basic Park History" and a "Historic Structure Report" to provide all possible data for the benefit of architects involved in any restoration plans. Later it was decided to give first priority to the latter report in order to expedite these plans.

Stinson researched exhaustively at libraries and archival repositories in Denver, Santa Fe, Saint Louis, Laramie, Berkeley, New Haven, and Washington, D.C., among other places, concentrating on the physical evidence offered by eye-witnesses. His excellent unpublished "Historic Structure Report, Reconstruction, Bent's Old Fort" was not completed until early 1966. It, coupled with Moore's archaeological report, became "the Bible" for the architects later assigned.[48]

---

[47] Superintendent to regional director, 24 July 1963; "Research Project Proposals Report," BOFS-NPS.

[48] Copies of Dwight E. Stinson, Jr., report at BOFS-NPS and Historic Preservation file, DSC-NPS. The notes and drawings of Lieutenant James W. Abert, 1846, were crucial to the successful synthesis of historical and archaeological data. Concerning the search for the original, *see* Mattes to W.E. Marshall, 13 May 1963, BOFS-NPS.

The archaeological project was a much bigger and more complex problem. Mattes and Logan came up with a cost estimate of nearly one hundred thousand dollars for a comprehensive dig, coupled with laboratory work and report preparation. This was a staggering unheard-of sum for such an undertaking, when compared to the few hundred hard dollars that went into the 1954 state investigation. Yet, miracles do occur, and in this case the NPS convinced the Bureau of the Budget and the two congressional subcommittees that this was a necessary investment. The required funds appeared in three, approximately equal, installments in fiscal years 1964, 1965, and 1966. The actual duration of the excavation phase, coinciding with "Smokey" Moore's assignment to the area, was September 1963 to July 1966.[49]

The published Moore report (1973) covers the impressive body of archaeological findings and conclusions. The site presented immense technical difficulties to the archaeologist, for here was a site with several occupational levels. True, the main features were of the Bent period, 1833 to 1849, but there was evidence of earlier occupation by both Indians and whites, then occupation by the stage company, later use as a corral by various early ranchers, and then the depredations of scores of souvenir hunters over the decades. Finally, there were complications resulting from the well-intentioned, state-sponsored project of 1954, which had one positive result, namely, to demonstrate that beneath the sand and the silt deposited by the Great Pueblo Flood of 1921 there was indeed substantial evidence of the original foundation walls. However, the technique employed in 1954, designed to explore maximum ground in a short period of time, had the unfortunate result that "less data were obtained in the later dig than could have been possible if the earlier one had not been made." More specifically, "evidence of the association of the walls with particular grade levels was destroyed. The technique also removed evidence of the presence or absence of builders' ditches." Also lacking was the provenance of the 1954 artifact assemblage.[50]

During the dig there was some turnover of labor personnel, but the average work force at any given time was no more than

---

[49] This and other data on the "Big Dig" are mainly derived from BOFS-NPS and progress reports, filed by Jackson W. Moore, Jr., with Wilfred Logan, Midwest Region (in his possession), DSC-NPS.

[50] Jackson W. Moore, Jr., *Bent's Old Fort: An Archeological Study*, (Denver and Boulder: State Historical Society of Colorado and Pruett Publishing Co., 1973), pp. 115-16.

In the aerial view, taken in November 1964, all of the floors are exposed, except for most of the long wagon room (left). In the south corner of the compound (below), archaeologists excavated material and cultural remains, evidence that helped explain the uses of the rooms.

six. On the other hand, thanks to clement winter weather and a blithe disregard of summer heat, the project continued with only brief interruptions around the calendar, in contrast to the usual dig that is a brief summertime affair. "Smokey" was on the job almost daily during his three-year stint.[51]

Over thirty-five thousand artifacts were collected. Laboratory and storage space was provided in a renovated shed left over from the Baldridge era, and the artifacts were carefully examined and analyzed by the archaeologist for his report. The mammoth job of conserving and cataloging the artifacts was performed mainly by Richard Carillo of La Junta. The NPS, recognizing the uniqueness of the collection, has placed it in Accountable Property.[52] The collection will be permanently stored in the reconstructed fort.

Unearthed during the NPS excavations, these bottles probably contained whiskey, bitters, and wine or champagne.

At first the exposed adobe remnants were allowed to weather because of optimism concerning early reconstruction. When it became evident that this would not happen for some years, it was recognized that the archaeological remains *in situ* should be protected to the extent possible. Spraying a polyurethene solution on all of the exposed walls and then covering them with soil cement and plywood shelters were not unmitigated successes. Weathering and ground-water capillary action triumphed over professional ingenuity. However, this was not a genuine disaster because of the fairly complete photographic records. Also, reconstruction along the lines of the original foundation walls would unavoidably obliterate all but a minute fraction of the surviving remnants.[53]

Meanwhile, more mundane matters of area operation required attention. In 1964 there was land clearing and seeding, and some doctoring up of the farm buildings for park operational use. In May 1965 Foy Young was transferred to Organ Pipe Cactus National Monument and Stinson filled in until August, when William Featherstone arrived from Washington, D.C., to become the superintendent.

"Bill" Featherstone was strong on public relations. In December 1965 he started contributing weekly columns to the *La Junta Tribune-Democrat* entitled "Report from Bent's Old Fort," in which he informed local citizens what was happening on the premises, what was cooking back in the region or in Washington, D.C., or simple tidbits of fort history. About this time the NPS unwisely abolished their traditional area monthly reports, leaving future historians stranded. The Featherstone column is therefore a godsend for it provides inside insights not available in the official files. Incidentally, when Featherstone was transferred to the Colorado State Office of the NPS in Denver in 1969, the column was kept up by Robert E. Davidson,

---

[51] Prior to the Bent's Old Fort project, Moore conducted excavations at Fort Smith in Arkansas, Fort Frederica and Ocmulgee in Georgia, and Franklin Court at Independence National Historical Park in Philadelphia. After a tour of duty in Omaha he was transferred to Washington, D.C., where he now serves as assistant chief archaeologist.

[52] Interview with Nan Rickey, DSC-NPS, September 1975 (hereinafter cited as Rickey Interview). Richard Carillo, then an Otero County Junior College student, is now an archaeologist with the staff of the University of South Carolina Institute of Archaeology and Anthropology. In 1967 a two-man team from the NPS Museum Laboratory in San Francisco spent two weeks at the site "to clean all rust and corrosion off the iron" (*Pueblo Chieftain*, 5 June 1967); property file, BOFS-NPS.

[53] Archaeological file, BOFS-NPS. The well and a portion of an interior wall section are the only remnants of the original fort that could be incorporated in the 1975-76 reconstruction. A program for the future archaeology of features outside of the fort proper, including dumps, ice-house, Santa Fe Trail alignment, cemetery, Indian campsites, race-track, etc., is set forth in a memorandum from Logan to Mattes, 18 October 1973, DSC-NPS.

who served also as acting superintendent until the arrival in May 1970 of the present superintendent, John R. Patterson, from Theodore Roosevelt Memorial Park. The editor reported that Featherstone and Davidson, between them, had contributed 223 articles up to that time, and bemoaned the fact that, with Davidson's transfer to Mount Rushmore, that would probably be the end of the column, which proved to be the case.[54]

Improvements prior to the present fort reconstruction were necessarily minor and temporary in character but they did represent conscientious efforts by park personnel to preserve and to interpret the fragile resource. Among efforts to improve the situation were the following: boundary surveys and fencing; parking area and road surfacing; exhibits in the laboratory shed; a small frame contact station manned by seasonal personnel; a trail to the riverside; restroom and picnic facilities; and, at the excavated fort site, panel exhibits, an audio message repeater, a free self-guiding tour leaflet, a fur-press replica, and gravel surfacing of the central plaza area. An unusual and most effective innovation by Patterson was the construction in 1972 of a temporary blacksmith shop with adobe walls and pole roof, constructed with the help of the Colorado Boys Ranch at La Junta. This and other devices and demonstrations helped to stimulate visitor interest during the long wait for reconstruction. That the superintendents succeeded in this goal is evidenced by attendance figures that peaked to forty thousand or more annually, despite the lack of much of anything to see at the area but the archaeological remnants, an odd configuration of low earthern mounds.[55]

During this period, three other projects engaged the attention of area and regional personnel, all related to the Arkansas River. First was a $5,000 project for the eradication of tamarisk or salt-cedar, a feathery desert plant up to ten feet high that threatened to take over the entire river bottom. The procedure was to blade this exotic species with a bulldozer, burn the dead plants, and apply herbicides to prevent recurrence. A second concern was the identification of historic meanders of the river to determine its stream bed during the historic period. Upon the request of the superintendent, the United States Geological

---

[54] Copies of occasional issues in data files, BOFS-NPS. The only known complete runs are in the La Junta newspaper office, and in newspaper files, SHSC.

[55] "Reports from Bent's Old Fort," and files, BOFS-NPS; "Bent's Old Fort Will Live Again," *Pueblo Star-Journal and Sunday Chieftain,* 21 July 1968; interviews with John R. Patterson and William Featherstone, September 1975. Visitors count in 1975 and 1976 exceeded 100,000.

Survey addressed itself to the problem. In USGS Professional
Paper 700-B (1970) hydrologist Frank A. Swensen, after several
pages of technical jargon, came up with the conclusion that,
"despite the fact that the Arkansas River, in the reach near
Bent's Old Fort, has well-developed meanders, and the river is
flowing on easily erodable material, there has been relatively
little shift of the stream since 1869," when first scientifically
mapped.[56]

A third concern was a 1967 proposal by the Albuquerque
District, Corps of Army Engineers, for the channelization of the
Arkansas River for flood control purposes. Regional Director
Fred Fagergren objected strongly to Colonel J.H. Hottenroth
that the scheme involving dikes would have a distinctly adverse
effect on the historic site, because in lieu of a natural river front,
there would be the unsightly dike structures. He pointed out
that here was the historic Santa Fe Trail Crossing of the Arkansas River and that here also at one time was the international
boundary with Mexico; furthermore, the engineers' proposal
would violate the Historic Preservation Act of 1966 as well as
the act creating the historic site. At the same time he agreed
that it would be well to protect the fort somehow from the
ravages of future floods, such as occurred in 1921 and 1965.[57] It
does not appear that any compromise in principle was reached.
The channelization project has since been put back on the shelf,
but there is no reason to think that this threat will not be
revived some day.

The NPS has been planning and replanning the future of
Bent's Old Fort since 1960, but not without the usual quota of
soul-searching, internal debate, and ground-shifting. The official planning device is the "Master Plan" and its auxiliary
"Interpretive Plan." There have been several versions of these
before the final ones that have now led straight to the completed
reconstruction.

It is ironic that, in the matter of reconstruction, the final
result is similar to that contained in the first plan for the fort
ever formulated. Identified as "Proposed Development Plan,"
this was put together by Hieb, Mattes, and others of the regional
staff in anticipation of the Enabling Act and was submitted by
Regional Director Baker to Director Wirth on 22 January 1960.

---

[56] "Reports from Bent's Old Fort," and USGS Professional Paper 700-B (1970), BOFS-NPS.

[57] Fred Fagergren to chief, Engineering Division, Corps of Engineers, Colonel J.H. Hottenroth,
Albuquerque, N. Mexico, 15 September, 29 September 1967, and 1 January 1968, BOFS-NPS.

In a memorandum of 17 March 1961 Baker repeated his request
for the director's approval of the plan:

> In view of the very complete documentary, pictorial and
> archaeological information available as to the dimensions,
> structural materials, and appearance of Bent's Old Fort c.
> 1846, a full scale reconstruction as of that period would be
> possible. Moreover, it is believed that such a reconstruction
> would be justified under the basic policy statement of the
> National Park Service on the restoration of historic struc-
> tures.
>
> The impressive external appearance of such a recon-
> structed fort in a restored setting . . . would . . . add greatly to
> visitor appreciation and understanding of the site. Moreover,
> internal treatment of the reconstruction presents a variety of
> possibilities. One or more large sections of the interior build-
> ings would be openly modernized for use as a visitor center, a
> few typical rooms would be accurately reconstructed and fur-
> nished as authentic full-scale exhibits, and in a few areas
> interesting remains . . . would be preserved . . . . By so combin-
> ing our visitor center with a reconstructed adobe fort the need
> for modern-appearing intrusions within a quarter-mile of the
> fort site would be limited to a parking area 100 yards to the
> northeast where variations in the terrain would render it least
> conspicuous. The present Baldridge house and equipment
> sheds would be used temporarily and all later employee quar-
> ters and utility buildings grouped . . . along Highway 194.[58]

This same basic scheme was echoed in the first formal "Master
Plan," put together by Don Rickey, Logan, and others, and
approved by Assistant Director Stratton in May 1963.[59]

There was some dissent from this format, but the principal
disruption came with the advent of a 1965 report by a four-man
"Committee to Review Western Forts' Interpretive Development Programs." The members consisted of two interpretive
experts from the Harper's Ferry (West Virginia) Center, one
historian from the Washington D.C., Office, and a retired chief
of interpretation with a naturalist background. The report was
not unanimous except in the matter of eliminating employee
housing from the area as environmentally objectionable. There
was majority agreement that there should be a visitor center
structure separate from the fort, because "the space and arrangement of the rooms in a reconstructed fort would not permit
a feasible visitor center function nor adequately provide office
space."

---

[58] BOFS-NPS.
[59] WASO-NPS, interview with Logan, DSC-NPS, September 1975.

This blue ribbon committee was split down the middle on the issue of reconstruction. Those opposing claimed that reconstruction would be highly conjectural and would obliterate authentic remains. Instead they proposed preservation of the ground-level ruins and an adjoining visitor center with overhanging roof. The two members in favor were quite emotional in defense of reconstruction. First, they affirmed that the approved Stinson report amply demonstrated that a reconstruction would be authentic and not conjectural. Second, they considered the archaeological remnants too meager to constitute an impressive display and furthermore there was no known method to ensure their preservation for posterity (except perhaps to build a big plastic dome over the whole fort area, which would horrify everybody). Finally, they appealed to the creative imagination of their audience:

> It should not be overlooked that there is nowhere in the System, nor is there ever likely to be, another historic structure, either original, restored or reconstructed, like Bent's Old Fort, should it be rebuilt .... It may be stated with full confidence that a reconstruction of Bent's Old Fort would constitute a unique educational, architectural, and historical exhibit of top rank in the United States. This alone argues powerfully for its reconstruction.[60]

Meanwhile, some Colorado citizens were getting into the act, concerned about delays resulting from planning dilemmas, and particularly about rumors of "no reconstruction." Early in 1966 Senator Peter H. Dominick inquired about the reconstruction issue on behalf of Charles E. Nelson, president of the Denver Chapter of the Colorado Archaeological Society, who "speaks for a large group of interested persons." Assistant Director Howard W. Baker (who had transferred from Omaha to the director's office in 1965) replied that "there had been no real stoppage in the work," what with various research programs, but that the evaluation of the data was not complete and the NPS was not yet "in a position to make a final decision on whether the information at hand will permit a reasonably accurate replica."[61] Since Baker had come out four-square for reconstruction in 1960 when he was regional director, this new hesitancy can be interpreted as a reflection of a strong tide, in the director's office at this time, running against reconstruction.

---

[60] Copies at BOFS-NPS and DSC-NPS.

[61] Interview with Allott, Denver, 6 January 1976 (hereinafter cited as Allott Interview); Baker to Peter H. Dominick, 9 February 1966, BOFS-NPS. On 4 October 1965 Mattes wrote to Regional Director Lou Garrison challenging a statement by Assistant Director Joseph Jensen to Allott that there were serious research problems.

In May 1966 William E. Marshall, executive director of the Society, wrote Superintendent Featherstone expressing concern about delays and pointing out that "we are obviously interested in the progress being made toward the restoration of Bent's Fort, and we are frequently asked about the situation." In reply, the superintendent frankly conceded that "the preliminary work has been done, but actual construction may not begin for several years yet. Many things enter into the delay, including the Service's own planning." Evidently Marshall concluded that it was time to blow the whistle on wobbly NPS planners, because the fall-out from this exchange was a stiff note early in 1967 from Senator Allott to the director, "Honorable George Hartzog," expressing impatience with procrastination about deciding whether or not the fort should be reconstructed, reminding the director that early in February 1966 he had been promised that a decision would be forthcoming. In late April 1967 Acting Director Harthon L. Bill wrote the senator, expressing regrets about the lengthy delay, owing to the fact that "the problem is unique because of the large adobe structure involved." Bill then reviewed the alternatives that had been posed by the Fort Study Team and then assured the senator that "the Service does intend to program the reconstruction within the range of these alternatives."[62]

In June Regional Director Fagergren urged a decision to reconstruct, "with the Visitor Center and administrative headquarters within the restored structure." On 17 August Acting Director Baker announced: "Our decision is to reconstruct." However, "a separate structure similar to our usual visitor centers in other areas will be built to provide the customary facilities needed for visitor comfort and general interpretive orientation." Baker further explained that incorporation of modern facilities in the historic structure would be "a short-sighted piece of planning that would not meet requirements" and would have the further disadvantage of "violating historic values in the reconstructed fort."[63]

After more painful introspection in Washington, D.C., Director Hartzog, in January 1968 confirmed the decision to rebuild the fort but at the same time to construct a separate Visitor Center adjacent to State Highway 194. He also re-

[62] W.E. Marshall to Featherstone, 27 May 1966; Featherstone to Marshall, 3 June 1966, CF-SHSC. Allott to George Hartzog, 31 March 1967; Harthon Bill to Allott, 28 April 1967, WASO-NPS.

[63] Fagergren to Baker, 14 June 1967, Baker to Fagergren, 17 August 1967, WASO-NPS.

affirmed that there would be no modern residences to clutter up the scenery; the employees could live in La Junta or elsewhere.[64] The director and his advisers may be given credit for planning wisdom in this case, but there is reason to believe that there were also political considerations. A decision not to reconstruct would have run counter to all earlier plans and might have resulted in so much consternation and objection among Coloradoans that it may well have been reversed in time. In all fairness to those skeptics among NPS planners, it should be emphasized, however, that neither the 1960 authorization bill nor statements by federal spokesmen prior to that date included any actual commitments to reconstruct.

Despite the "Great Decision" there was still no construction money in sight, which did have the advantage of allowing leeway for more agonizing reappraisal. The final turning point came in 1971 with an interpretive planning team headed by Nan Rickey of the Harper's Ferry Center. In her report the separate Visitor Center was once more discarded, and all functions, historical and managerial, were put back into the big mud fort so that visitors would not be distracted by anything that might hamper the illusion that they were back in 1846, visiting William Bent's marvelous emporium.[65] The Washington, D.C., Office's favorable review of her plan, three years after announcing plans for a separate Visitor Center, was probably influenced by sober economic as well as aesthetic considerations. After all, where is the logic in building two, large structures if you can get by with one? Presumably the once influential objections of the Fort Study Team were now considered frivolous and invalid. So with the final approval of her report, the main thrust of development was crystallized.

Now the only problem left was the perennial one of money. When would that famous reconstruction project, first dimly envisioned by the DAR Chapter in 1920, achieve form and substance? It does not appear that the Midwest Regional Office was delinquent in requesting funds for design and construction. Starting in 1969 such requests appeared regularly in *preliminary* budgets but never quite made it to the *final* budget, after pruning by the director, the secretary, or the White House under the severe economic pressures of the Viet Nam War,

---

[64] Featherstone, "Report from Bent's Old Fort," *La Junta Tribune-Democrat,* 25 June 1968. That year a utility building was constructed in the northwest corner of the area, adjacent to State Highway 194. Screened by trees, it is not conspicuous from the fort.

[65] Rickey Interview, September 1975.

burgeoning welfare programs, and recessions.[66] All of the evidence indicates that Bent's Old Fort would not have been reconstructed in 1975-76 if it had not been for the diligent and the persistent efforts of certain Colorado congressmen, spurred on by leaders of the Society. In fact, this became a patriotic campaign, the keynote of which was sounded by Society Executive Director Marshall in a memorandum of 23 February 1972 to Society President Walter A. Steele:

> The executive committee agreed that the Historical Society should ask its Congressmen to attempt to persuade the National Park Service to adjust its priorities so as to begin reconstruction of Bent's Old Fort as quickly as possible — as a contribution to the Nation's Bicentennial, but more specifically, as a worthwhile contribution to Colorado's Centennial.[67]

In April Steele wrote Senator Dominick, bringing to his attention "a long overdue, urgently needed historic reconstruction effort of the National Park Service in Colorado." He pointed out that when state land was transferred by the legislature in 1961,"it was felt at that time that the reconstruction would be given a high priority," but "somehow this worthwhile project has become lost on the list."[68] That same month Stephen H. Hart, now chairman of the Society's Board of Directors, addressed Rogers C. B. Morton, secretary of the interior, in the same vein. He described the fort as

> a very important historical, educational and tourist resource . . . . [Its] reconstruction would be one of the nation's most distinguished historic projects. It was promised many years ago by the National Park Service . . . . It is my personal opinion that a proper reconstruction . . . . in the superb manner that the National Park Service does its job would be a tremendous attraction and inspiration, a preeminent one actually rivalling Pike's Peak or Rocky Mountain National Park in Colorado. It would . . . . be possible, if acted upon promptly, to do the work in time for the National Bicentennial Celebration . . . It would involve no expense beyond that to which the National Park Service is ultimately committed.[69]

To ensure that all parties in a position to be influential got the message, both gentlemen sent copies of their pleas to Col-

---

[66] From 1969 through 1971 Mattes, as chief, Office of History and Historic Architecture, Western Service Center, San Francisco, worked with the midwest regional director and staff on programming all preservation projects.

[67] Marshall to Walter A. Steele, 23 February 1972, CF-SHSC.

[68] Steele to Dominick, 3 April 1972, CF-SHSC.

[69] Stephen H. Hart to Rogers C.B. Morton, 19 April 1972, CF-SHSC.

orado members of Congress; Senators Allott and Dominick, Representatives Wayne H. Aspinall, Donald G. Brotzman, James D. McKevitt, and Frank E. Evans; likewise, Governor John A. Love, Floyd Sack, and Joe Albi, officers of the Colorado Centennial-Bicentennial Commission. This resulted in a bombardment of letters to Secretary Morton and Director Hartzog requesting clarification of construction plans, and "why no appropriations have been sought for the fort." Frank Evans, representing the Arkansas River valley constituency, advised Hart that, in a telephone conversation with an unidentified official, "the Service assured me that they are placing on their timetable concrete steps for the accomplishment of reconstruction in Fiscal 1975. In addition, I have written the Director emphasizing my hope that this time-table will not be delayed.[70]

When it came down to cash on the line, to get the project actually off dead center, it appears that Senator Gordon Allott should get most of the credit. He first ascertained that a four-year development schedule prepared by the NPS "calls for a total expenditure of $1.4 million, with $50,000 required in the first year. If the initial development funds are provided in F.Y. '73, the Park Service contemplates completion of the reconstruction by '76." Then the senator learned that the $50,000 the NPS originally requested for preliminary design work had been blue-penciled, as usual, by the administration, and it had not been restored by the House Interior Appropriations Subcommittee.[71] He then went to work, in time-honored fashion, on his fellow members of the Senate Appropriation Committee. It was with understandable triumph, therefore, that on 26 June 1972, he wired Hart as follows:

> AM PLEASED TO ANNOUNCE THAT THE SENATE APPROPRIATIONS COMMITTEE APPROVED MY AMENDMENT OF $50,000 TO COMMENCE RECONSTRUCTION OF BENT'S OLD FORT. THE FUNDS INCLUDED IN THIS BILL WILL INITIATE A FOUR-YEAR SCHEDULE WITH COMPLETION TO COINCIDE WITH THE COLORADO STATE CENTENNIAL IN 1976. I AM HOPEFUL THAT THE SENATE WILL PREVAIL IN RETAINING THESE FUNDS DURING CONFERENCE WITH THE HOUSE.[72]

[70] Hart to James D. McKevitt, 19 April; McKevitt to Hart, 27 April; Hart to Allott, 19 April; Allott to Hart, 27 April; Evans to Hart, 19 April; Evans to Hartzog, 19 April 1972, Office files, Stephen H. Hart (hereinafter cited as OF-Hart).

[71] Allott to Senator Alan Bible, 2 May 1972, CF-SHSC; Allott Interview, 6 January 1976.

[72] OF-Hart.

Conclusive proof, if any was needed, that Senator Allott, and not any government officials, was responsible for this breakthrough lies in the record. Only days before the senator's telegram was sent, these officials were lamely explaining that their four-year plan had been delayed indefinitely for lack of funds.[73]

On 5 July Senator Dominick wrote to Hart echoing joy in the success of "Gordon's Amendment" but cautioning that "now we will have to tangle with the House when we meet in joint conference." Leaving no stone unturned, he then identified the Senate conferees: "It's just a thought, but you might like to contact them." Meanwhile, Donald Brotzman and Frank Evans polled conferees of the House of Representatives, and Senator Allott touched base with Julia Butler Hansen, the influential chairman of the House Interior Subcommittee.[74] On 27 July the senator sent Hart a second triumphant wire:

> THE JOINT CONFERENCE COMMITTEE APPROVED THE SENATE RECOMMENDATION OF 50,000 TO COMMENCE RECONSTRUCTION OF BENT'S OLD FORT. NEEDLESS TO SAY I AM PLEASED THAT FUNDS WILL BE AVAILABLE NOW TO INITIATE THE SCHEDULE FOR PLANNED COMPLETION TO COINCIDE WITH THE COLORADO STATE CENTENNIAL IN 1976.[75]

The importance of this modest amendment tacked on to the Interior Appropriations Bill cannot be overestimated. Without it, there was no way the fort could be reconstructed by the Centennial Year. With it, as Hart, Gordon Allott, and the National Park Service well knew, the Congress had now assumed a moral obligation to complete the project.

The precious $50,000 was entrusted to the new Denver Service Center, which had been created in November 1971 by putting together the old Washington, D.C., and San Francisco Service Centers, to handle all research, planning, design, and contruction work nationwide. One branch of the center was the so-called Historic Preservation Team, and it devolved upon this group of specialists to get cracking on the Bent's Old Fort reconstruction plans. By coincidence the Team Manager Merrill J. Mattes was the same who, years before as midwest chief of

[73] Morton to Hart, 16 June 1972, CF-SHSC.

[74] Dominick to Hart, 5 July; Hart to Dominick, 11 July; Donald G. Brotzman to George Mahon, 17 July 1972, CF-SHSC; Allott Interview, 6 January 1976.

[75] CF-SHSC.

history and archaeology, had helped lay the groundwork for the
original fort research, planning and programming, a rare instance of project continuity. Because the team was so short-
handed, it was decided to go to contract for the design work and
the construction drawings. This contract was awarded to the
Ken R. White Company, a planning, engineering, and architectural firm of Denver, in the amount of $59,122, making it neces-
sary to supplement the appropriated amount with reserve
funds. George Thorson of that company was the principal architect on the project. Thomas R. Jones, senior historical architect of the Denver Service Center and specialist in adobe
construction, was project coordinator. The design documents
were submitted in October 1973.[76]

In fiscal 1974 the respectable sum of $300,000 was appro-
priated by Congress for the reconstruction of the fort, after the
customary economy game the fort's proponents had learned how
to play — budget insertions, deletions, and reinsertions by Senate action. Of this amount $229,000 was released by the
Washington, D.C., Office to the Denver Service Center. The
Historic Preservation Team politely pointed out that this was
not nearly enough to reconstruct the fort or even to warrant a
start on reconstruction.[77] This was the approximate amount
estimated originally, in 1961, on the basis of preliminary·design
work at that time by architect Robert Gann of the old Western
Office, Design and Construction, San Francisco. In 1965 engineers of the Washington, D.C., Office had calculated a cost of
$600,000. In 1967 the Regional Office had upped the amount to
$700,000. With construction costs escalating since then it was
no great surprise that Denver Service Center estimators in 1974
figured that basic construction costs would be in the range of
$1,500,000, and utilities, furnishings, and related site develop-
ment would bring the total to over $2,000,000![78]

By this time another of the frequent reorganizations that
convulse the National Park Service took place. One result of a
drastic regional realignment was the creation of a new Rocky

[76] DSC-NPS, David E. Nichols, Ken R. White Company, to Mattes, DSC, 15 October 1973.

[77] DSC-NPS. Although documentation is lacking, conversations with the staff of Congressman
   Frank E. Evans and with personnel of the Rocky Mountain Regional Office suggests that Evans
   was quite instrumental in securing the $300,000 in this second round of financing the project.

[78] DSC-NPS; Utley to the midwest regional director, 18 January 1967; data derived from "Project
   Construction Proposal B-8 (revised)," 28 July 1965; Fagergren to director, 14 June 1967, with
   construction estimates, WASO-NPS; this impressive figure is a few light years away, so to speak,
   from the modest sums discussed by state and local officials twenty years before. Inflation is not
   the main factor in this seeming cost explosion. The main factor is the totality of the National Park
   Service restoration goal, far beyond anything previously contemplated.

Mountain Region, with headquarters in Denver. Bent's Old Fort, so long the hope and despair of the old Midwest Region, suddenly found itself in this new region, and it became the duty of new Regional Director Lynn H. Thompson and his staff to seek this rather formidable funding if Bent's Old Fort was to be reconstructed by the Centennial Year.

At the same time the director was being posted about the awkward financial bind, permission was sought and granted for the Historic Preservation Team to utilize a portion of the $229,000 to proceed with design work and drawings for the total area development, including utilities, parking entrances, visitor facilities, signs, trails, and other items. This led to a supplemental contract with Ken R. White in the amount of $27,742. The completed drawings and specifications for the basic structure were delivered on 18 April 1974 and approved on 7 June.[79] Meanwhile Thorson was hired by the NPS as a contract supervisor for the Historic Preservation Team, thus enabling him to continue with the construction phase of the fort. During this same period, in anticipation of the need for detailed furnishing of the historic structure in contemporary style, contracts were awarded successively to Enid Thompson and Sarah Olson, both Denver residents, for furnishings studies and plans, which would become the basis for the curatorial work.

Now there remained the small matter of the missing $2,000,000. Despite the eloquent pleas of the Rocky Mountain Region, this particular construction item did not appear in the final 1975 NPS budget, part of the Interior Department Appropriation Bill. The horrendous cost of official bicentennial projects on the Eastern seaboard, coupled with the usual chief executive office pressures to keep the lid on spending, conspired to thwart the consummation of the dream cherished by Otero County, indeed all of Colorado, of a resurrected fort. Then what happened to bring about the reversal and the final victory?

There was no fairy godmother with a magic wand. But there were a few Coloradoans in a position of influence who refused to accept this frustration. To reduce this story to its fundamentals, key personnel of the Society and the Colorado Centennial-Bicentennial Commission, having been briefed on the problem by the regional director and the manager of the Historic Preservation Team at the Denver Service Center, carried a vigorous campaign to the doorsteps of the Colorado congressional delega-

[79] DSC-NPS.

tion, principally Senator Peter H. Dominick and Representative Frank E. Evans of the Third District, although the help of Floyd Haskell, Patricia Schroeder, Donald Brotzman, and others was enlisted also. Here was one issue on which politicians of all shades of opinion could join. The old fort is practically Colorado's number one historic shrine and these people were determined that, after fifteen years of waiting, the Centennial-Bicentennial Year was "the moment of truth."

The story of the last push over the last big hump is brief though somewhat spectacular. Learning that the fort construction money was missing from the Interior Department Appropriations Bill, as passed by the House, Stephen H. Hart, chairman of the Board of Directors of the Society, once more took up his pen, this time concentrating on Senator Dominick, since the Senate Interior Appropriations Subcommittee was now the last hope. The senator was not a member of this committee nor of the whole Senate Committee on Appropriations, and the details of his maneuvering by the various processes of "button-holing," "cloakroom" conferences, and debate from the Senate floor are lacking. All that is known is that on 27 June 1974 he issued a news release about his request for $2.3 million for Bent's Old Fort, and on 12 August he informed his constituents that the full Senate had approved this item. On 31 August President Gerald Ford signed the Interior Department Appropriations Bill, which retained the full amount.[80]

Hart, who has been associated with the Society's program for the fort longer than anybody else of that organization, undoubtedly was the prime mover in enlisting strong congressional interest in getting the crucial money bills passed. His wife, Lorna, who in 1974 was chairman of the Heritage Council of the Colorado Centennial-Bicentennial Commission, traveled to Washington, D.C., in April 1974 and also played a significant role in motivating the congressmen. Hart definitely agrees with conclusions apparent also from the documentary evidence, that two Colorado senators played pivotal roles that posterity must recognize — Gordon Allott in securing the original $50,000 in construction funds, which was the key to initiating the entire development, and Peter Dominick for his success in securing the $2 million to ensure 1976 completion at a time when this item had been erased from the official budget.[81]

[80] Hart to Dominick, 5 April 1974, CF-SHSC; OF-Hart; *Denver Post,* 1 September 1974.

[81] Interview with Stephen H. Hart, 5 January 1976 (hereinafter cited as Hart Interview).

Gordon Allott should also be remembered as the one most responsible for congressional acceptance of the establishment of the fort as a National Historic Site in the first place, for lining up federal funds for the purchase of private lands, and for demanding NPS resolution of planning dilemmas. Aside from "politics" the senator was motivated by a sincere desire to "save Bent's Fort," having lived in Lamar from 1930 until his election to the Senate in 1954 and having observed the deterioration of the fort and other sites in that vicinity.[82]

Frank E. Evans, the champion of the Arkansas River valley in the House of Representatives and the man who laid the first adobe brick in the ceremony of 5 July 1975, was a staunch supporter of the fort legislation. He is credited with a major role in the 1972 and 1974 appropriation struggles. It should be noted also that he was a key member of the Colorado General Assembly when transfer of the site to the federal government was authorized in 1961.[83]

Prior to the award of the reconstruction contract, two formalities had to be taken care of. First was the clearance of the project by the State Preservation Officer and the Advisory Council on Historic Preservation, in accordance with the Historic Preservation Act of 1965, relating to federal properties. Second was the approval of an updated "master plan/interpretive prospectus/development concept plan/environmental assessment," hopefully "final" after fifteen years of planning and replanning. The first posed no difficulties, particularly since the state official in question was the same Stephen H. Hart of the Society who had long been the number one advocate of reconstruction. The second was a mere technicality since the main elements, as far as reconstruction was concerned, had been settled since 1972, and the rest consisted mainly of interpretive refinements, which could be considered "frosting on the cake."[84]

All who have visited the project have marveled at the detailed authenticity of adobe bricks, mud plastering, vigas, stairways, hearths, rooms, towers, passageways, and the

[82] Allott Interview, 6 January 1976.

[83] Hart Interview, 5 January 1976, *La Junta Tribune-Democrat*, 7 July 1975.

[84] Richard Strait, Rocky Mountain Region, to Hart, 15 October 1974, BOFS-NPS; John D. McDermott, Office of Review and Compliance, Advisory Council on Historic Preservation, Washington, D.C., to Lynn H. Thompson, Rocky Mountain Region, 3 April 1975, CF-SHSC; Glenn T. Bean, Rocky Mountain Region, to Governor Richard D. Lamm, 25 March 1975, concerning "public meeting on the proposed reconstruction," 10 April 1975 at La Junta; Lamm to Thompson, 18 April 1975; Bean to Lamm, 6 May 1975, BOFS-NPS.

impressive character and credibility of the whole effort. It reflects thorough research, ingenious architectural design, and the touch of master craftsmen and builders who take pride in their accomplishments. Call it a reconstruction if you want to be technical, but to those who waited so long, as well as amateur and professional historians alike, it is truly a resurrection.

MERRILL J. MATTES, recipient of a United States Department of the Interior Distinguished Service Award, is the author of THE GREAT PLATTE RIVER ROAD *and many other books and articles on western history. A graduate of the University of Missouri, he received the M.A. degree from the University of Kansas and pursued graduate study at Yale University. Mattes's last assignment in his long association with the National Park Service was as chief of the Office of History and Historic Architecture at the Denver Service Center. He is now a free-lance historical writer and consultant.*

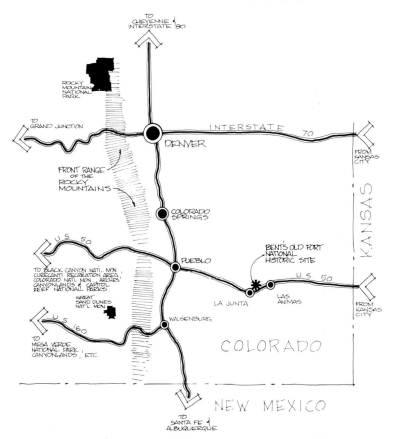

The Architectural Challenge

BY GEORGE A. THORSON

Spanish Americans from Taos have been brought up here, where the Santa Fe Trail crosses the Arkansas River to begin its southward thrust, to help build the fort – now making and laying adobes; logging cottonwoods, stripping their bark, and hoisting them in place; building doors, windows, and stairs. Anglos conceived the design, influenced by the adobe architecture that they were familiar with in New Mexico. Now they are in charge of construction, directing the blacksmith in the making of hardware and candle fixtures. There have been many delays getting started. It took time to gather enough funds to hire the workers and to buy materials from the East. It has not been easy to find the right trees, ones that were straight enough and of sufficient size to span the adobe walls. Finding the right adobe has been a problem also. But now the castle-like structure with its corner bastions is progressing well and will be finished by the summer.

This eyewitness account of the reconstruction of Bent's Old Fort is imaginary; it is not a page from a traveler's journal of the early 1830s, the time of the original construction of the fort. This account reflects conditions in early 1976, Colorado's Centennial and the nation's Bicentennial — the year of the completion of the historical reconstruction project of the National Park Service (NPS).

The major objective of the Bent's Old Fort Bicentennial Project, initiated by a federal appropriation of $50,000 for design work in 1972, was the reconstruction of the fort primarily as a historical exhibit. The only nonhistorical element was to be the wagon house that would be used as the staff area and also house the mechanical equipment and the restrooms.

The rationale for the reconstruction of the fort was compelling despite the admittedly high cost of such a project.[1] The original, fragile adobe had been subjected to the erosion of weather, the ravages of floods, and the salvaging of materials by neighbors. Only ground-level ruins remained to mark the place. Efforts to preserve these had largely failed, and soon even the token remains of the fort would be gone, melting back into the earth from which they came.

The argument for reconstruction in this case, then, was two-dimensional. Architecturally, there was a long held conviction that the mere preservation of the surviving archaeological remains, even if technologically possible, would scarcely inspire onlookers. And, secondly, pictures and models of the fort in a nearby modern museum structure would be a poor substitute for the full scale re-creation of this unique symbol of western expansion in American history.

The 1972 plan also anticipated 150,000 visitors per year. When seasonal factors were considered, this worked out to approximately 1,000-per-day or a maximum of 200-per-hour on a normal daily schedule. The visitor-use patterns certainly would affect the total project design, including parking, foot-traffic flow, restrooms, safety requirements, and other elements of the whole experience. The resultant "human erosion of the resource" would be easier to cope with in a reconstruction, where damage from public use could be rectified by rebuilding.

---

[1] The three major types of preservation projects are: preservation, sometimes called stabilization, which involves measures to ensure structure survival; restoration of a structure involving new construction of missing, original elements; and reconstruction, where a lost structure is rebuilt. The NPS places primary emphasis on preservation. Restoration is employed less frequently, and reconstruction is resorted to rarely because of the expense and the requirement of authenticity.

A full-scale reconstruction on site would, of course, destroy most, if not all, of the meager remaining evidence. So before the final and irretrievable commitment to reconstruction, the question of preserving any portion of the archaeological remains was carefully considered.

By 1972 the exposed ruins, including layers superimposed by the abortive State Historical Society of Colorado project of 1957, were only about one foot above grade. Pencapsula, a preservation chemical, was first sprayed on the adobe. It had worked elsewhere, but at Bent's Old Fort it penetrated less than one-half inch, created a water vapor film, and then popped off the outer adobe layer. Next, a concrete grout cover was applied, but the erosion continued. The third approach was to construct low wood shelters over the more critical ruins. Erosion persisted, presumably the result of capillary action of subterranean water, accentuated by nearby agricultural irrigation and the ill-advised watering of grass around the fort. Possibly a complicated drainage system to keep out the water would have worked, but it was too late and too expensive.

What little was left of the original trapezoid-shaped fort would be mainly sacrificed for an authentic and imposing reconstruction. But was there any original remnant that could be preserved, somehow, as an exhibit incorporated within the new construction? That question was answered with two sections of low adobe wall that were identified for special preservation and marked for display. One was to be in the northeast bastion, the other was in room 113, identified as a pantry.

This long-vanished adobe structure was to be reconstructed to its appearance circa 1845-46. These were the climactic years in frontier history, when William Bent's massive adobe trading post in southeastern Colorado became a focal point in events leading to the Mexican War and takeover of the New Mexico Territory, making it a significant factor in the explosive expansion of the United States to the Southwest and California. At this period, after additions and remodeling, the fort was at the peak of its physical development as well as its historical importance.

Besides its historical significance, the fort was architecturally unique; it represented the first major adobe structure of the Southwest designed by and for Anglos. With its corner bastions providing lookout firing positions along the walled enclosure, it was entitled to be called a fort, and its impressive facade had a military air about it. However, its interior was designed primarily to serve its major function —trade. The style and the construction techniques were basically Spanish Colonial, but the function of the fort was to serve the American commercial enterprise.

This, then, is the architectural story of the three challenges to *research, design,* and *construct* a building that would be as authentic as possible in every detail and would provide visitors with a time-space trip back to 1846. At the same time, durability was a requirement in the construction of the fort — to make it last 100 years or more in contrast to the 16-year lifespan of the original fort. The twin requirements of authenticity and durability had seemingly inherent contradictions that could be solved only with creative ingenuity to achieve a delicate yet convincing design balance.

During the latter part of 1972 and early 1973 the scope of the required architectural services was developed by the NPS. The services were to be performed in four phases: preliminary surveys and research, preliminary design, drawings and specification, and construction contracting.

Negotiations for the architectural services were held with the Ken R. White Company of Denver, and the initial contract was executed on 17 July 1973. The range of this contract included all professional aid and supporting activities for research, design, and construction documents for the reconstruction of the fort buildings. It included all necessary architectural, structural, electrical, plumbing, heating and air-conditioning, and fire and burglar detection systems. Site development and utilities were to be included in a second contract.

The central responsibility for the technical direction and the execution of the project belonged to the Historic Preservation Team at the Denver Service Center, under the direction of Team Manager Merrill J. Mattes. This was an assemblage of historical architects, historians, archaeologists, and various technicians, the largest such group in the NPS, which during this period was concerned with hundreds of projects nationwide, including those on the eastern seaboard related to the American Revolution Bicentennial celebrations.[2] T. Russell Jones, senior historical architect and a specialist in the adobe architecture of the Southwest, was assigned as consultant manager for the

---

[2] Other Denver Service Center units involved were Finance, Contracts, Engineering, and Interpretive Planning; the Harpers Ferry Center in West Virginia was concerned with interpretive installations; and the Rocky Mountain Regional Office in Denver was in charge of park operations.

project, as he had been the architect on such projects as the restoration of the Spanish Mission, Nuestra Senora de Guadalupe de Zuni, located at Zuni Pueblo in western New Mexico.

Following the acceptance of the initial contract, an orientation meeting was held on 23 July 1973 to finalize the initial concepts, objectives, and procedures of the project. Researching became the first critical task. The architects met with former area historian Dwight Stinson in the fall of 1973. During his two years in the La Junta area, Stinson had compiled all of the known history of the fort operations, buildings, people, and their activities — a combined area history and historic structure report. This compendium of data was synthesized into a comprehensive, unpublished report.

The architects were interested in all of the details regarding the structure and the life styles that would shed light on the fort's uses. No company records survived, but there were written descriptions by at least twenty-five primary eyewitnesses, a surprisingly large number considering the prevailing illiteracy of the period. These statements gave clues to the general appearance of the fort, the facilities and their use, and sometimes actual dimensions or materials. As expected the data was far from complete and puzzles abounded. Bent's Old Fort was built "by guess and by God," by experienced amateurs. There was no architect nor engineer to provide posterity with "as built" drawings and specifications. There were, of course, no photogaphs. A few unreliable drawings were sketched from memory many years later by George Bent and William Boggs. The Bent draw-

George Bent's 1908 sketch of the fort, made for George Bird Grinnell.

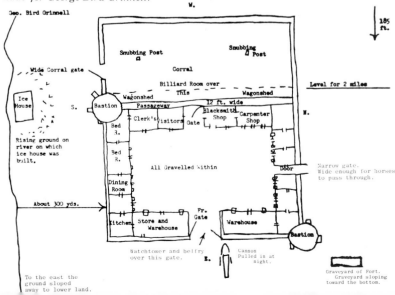

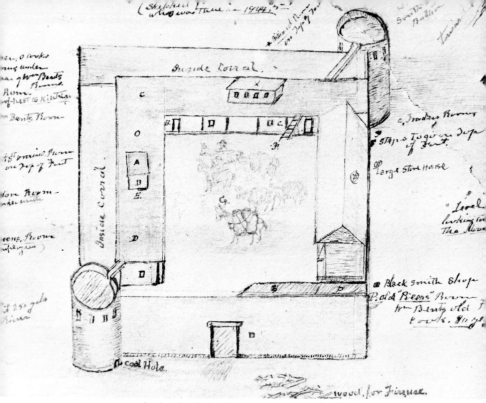

A sketch of the fort from memory by William M. Boggs.

ing relied on his memory as a six-year-old in 1849, and the
Boggs sketches recalled the fort from 1844 to 1849 when he was
a trader there.

The originals of Lieutenant James W. Abert's famous diary
and sketches were found by a connoisseur of Western
Americana, Fred Rosenstock of Denver.[3] This was the timely
breakthrough the architects had been looking for. Abert was a
"Renaissance Man" of his time and place, a twenty-six-year-old
military topographic engineer mapping the West as an aide to
General Stephen Watts Kearny. But he was also a naturalist; a
good writer; an artist who depicted Indians; and an engineer
who sketched buildings. He was laid up with "fever" at Bent's
Old Fort for one month in August 1846. As he was recovering,
and just before he left, he made sketches with dimensions that
were found on the margins and on the back of a watercolor
portrait of a Cheyenne Indian Chief, Ah-Mah-Nah-Co. They
included four views of the interior of the plaza, an entrance
elevation, and the overall roof plan of the fort. Although complicated by the divergent reports of eyewitnesses, some very obvi-

---

[3] Abert's diary and sketches were edited by John Galvin of Ireland and published in 1970 in two
editions for the years 1845 and 1846 by the John Howell Bookstore of San Francisco, California.

ous errors and fabrications, and, of course, the many hiatuses in the record, the historical data provided roughly thirty percent of the necessary material.

The architects also studied the comprehensive archaeological manuscript report, completed by Jackson W. Moore, Jr., in December 1964. This report contained details of the project beyond those supplied in Moore's published report. On 24 July 1973 the architects met with the archaeologist at the site of the ruins to gain further insights from his archaeology logs, notebooks, and plans.

The archaeological findings provided specific data regarding the foundation ground plan; floor surfaces and levels; structural framing patterns of the viga beams; adobes, mud plaster, and

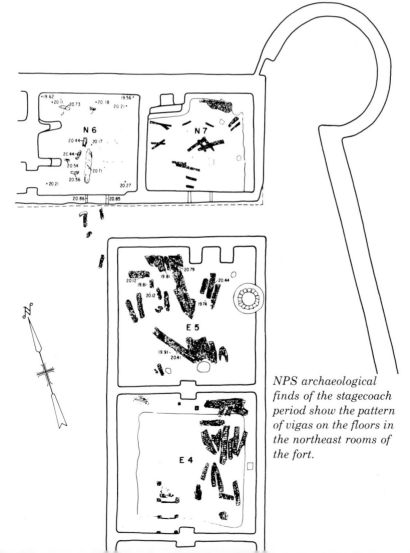

NPS archaeological finds of the stagecoach period show the pattern of vigas on the floors in the northeast rooms of the fort.

wall colors and finishes; hardware, guns, glass, bottles, skeletons, and other artifacts; and generally the most crucial physical evidence. The archaeological data, analyzed on a room-by-room basis, provided actual findings or the basis for conjectural interpretations. This procedure established the firm location of walls, posts, stairways, fireplaces and hearths, pits, wells, trenches, and other features. The artifacts, thus, gave clues to the use of the various rooms.

Archaeology could not supply all of the answers. Erosion, floods, roads, and agricultural activities had obliterated much of the evidence. Trinidad State Junior College excavators under Dr. Herbert W. Dick lacked the time and the resources to do more than a preliminary exploration in 1954, which itself posed some interpretive problems for later NPS archaeologists. Of course, no archaeology could identify any above-ground evidence except for collapsed materials, which were only fragmentary. The archaeological findings were, nevertheless, immensely valuable, representing an estimated thirty percent of the required architectural data. With the historical documentary data providing the other thirty percent, this left an estimated forty percent of the total body of data to be supplied by architectural studies.

In 1973 George Thorson and T. Russell Jones opened the architectural research phase.[4] After absorbing all of the hard data revealed by history and archaeology, a study of comparative data of other adobe buildings of this period was required to ascertain construction methods and details. The architects made a research tour of adobe structures in New Mexico in July 1973. Of particular interest were the pueblos at Zuni, Acoma, and Taos, along with the ancient adobe structures in Santa Fe and Taos. The Historic American Building Surveys drawings of New Mexico architecture of the 1930s were examined. Meetings were held with other architects, historians, manufacturers, and contractors familiar with modern adobe construction. A modern adobe reproduction of Bent's Old Fort, the Fort Restaurant near Morrison outside of Denver, was studied for its adobe construction technique. The State Historical Society of Colorado museum was visited. An open diorama of the fort, which had been made there years before, was an artistic one, but the architectural layout was based on limited data. The Western History Department of the Denver Public Library held addi-

---

[4] An NPS architect was scheduled to research the architectural section in 1966; however, funds were cut off and only preliminary sketches of the fort were completed.

The Society diorama of the fort was built in 1954.

tional sources that were helpful. And, work sessions on research and design problems were held with the many professional specialists at the Denver Service Center.

The combined input from all of these sources resulted in the development of a hypothetical description of the fort as it appeared in 1846. The fort was divided into four main areas: the compound, the inner corral, the wagon room, and the main corral. The compound was essentially a rectangular core of buildings (115 feet by 135 feet) around an inner plaza (80 feet by 90 feet). The inner corral on the east was a wedge-shaped area about 10 feet wide at the northeast bastion, expanding to 40 feet wide at the south. A 15-foot alley separated the compound from the 20-foot wagon house on the south and the 27-foot diameter bastion on the southwest corner. Therefore, the main fort was about 130 feet on the north front and 180 feet on the south with a 175-foot depth. Behind to the south was the main corral at 150 feet by approximately 140 feet (the precise dimension was lost due to earth disturbance). Twenty-nine rooms were identified on the lower level and 9 on the upper level. The enclosed rooms encompassed almost 17,000 square feet. The overall fort proper covered over 27,000 square feet, and the outer corral covered 21,000 square feet for a total of over 48,000 square feet, well over 1 acre. This was a large structure for that period, unlike anything else along the Santa Fe Trail or anything in Santa Fe itself.

The layout and the dimensions of the fort were set factually by archaeological data. However, the exact thickness of the original walls, obscured by erosion, was uncertain. Research had ascertained the dimension of the original adobes to be 18 inches by 9 inches by 4 inches; from this, exterior wall thicknesses were calculated to vary from 1.8 to 2.5 feet. Although Abert's roof plan drawings are the most reliable source of non-

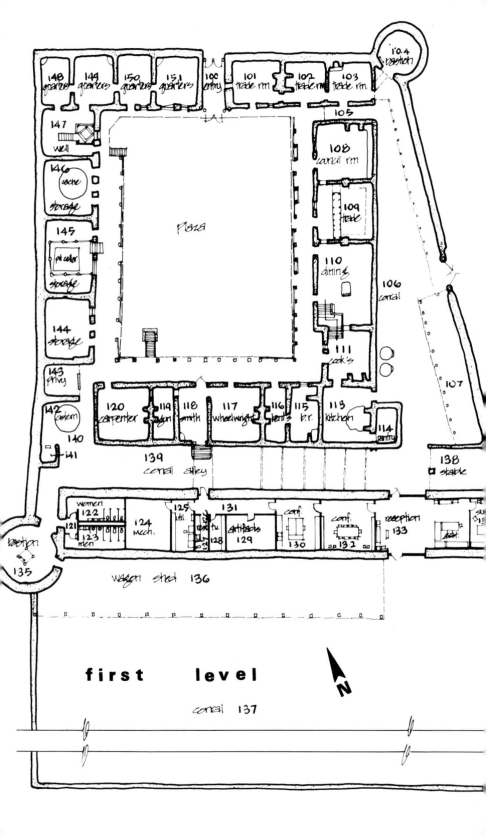

148 quarters
149 quarters
150 quarters
151 quarters
100 entry
101 trade rm
102 trade rm
103 trade rm
104 bastion
105
108 corral rm
109 trade
110 dining
106 corral
111 cook's
107
147 well
146 cache storage
145 pit cellar storage
144 storage
143 privy
142 cistern
140
141
Plaza

120 carpenter
119 ag rm
118 smith
117 wheelwright
116 clerk's b.r.
115
113 kitchen
114 sentry
138 stable
139 corral alley

122 women
121
123 men
124 mech.
125 util.
128
129 artifacts
131
130 conf.
132 conf.
133 reception
135 bastion
136 wagon shed

first   level

corral 137

N

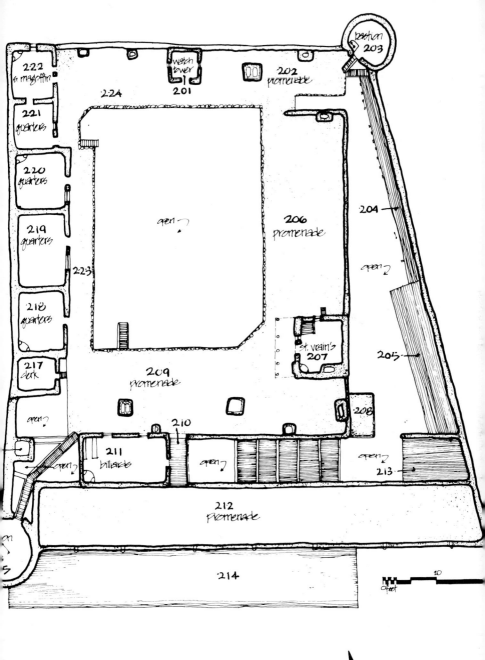

222
& magoffin

221
quarters

220
quarters

219
quarters

223

218
quarters

217
clerk

open?

open?

211
billiards

open?

224

watch
tower
201

open?

209
promenade

210

212
promenade

214

202
promenade

bastion
203

204

open?

205

206
promenade

st. vrain's
207

208

open?

213

open?

0 feet   10

second   level

N

archaeological information, some discrepancies became apparent. For example, he shows both bastions to be 27 feet in diameter; archaeological evidence shows the southwest bastion at 27 feet but the northeast bastion to be only 20 feet. (Presumably Lieutenant Abert, who was only doing it for his own use, measured only one bastion and assumed the other was the same.) The exterior vertical wall dimensions were given by Abert, and from these, logical heights for interior rooms were calculated.

Concurrent with the historic architectural research, studies were done on materials and fabric in the laboratory and in the field. The most important study was on adobe — one of man's first building materials since the Neolithic Period about 7,000 B.C. and still used in dry climates all over the world.[5] In reviewing the history of adobe in the New World, it was discovered that the Spanish explorers found the Indians of the arid Southwest making adobe by the "puddle method." The Spanish taught the Indians to make brick units, a faster and easier method of

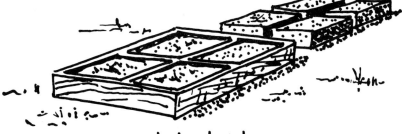

adobe bricks

construction. This technique, which became known as the Spanish Colonial Style, or Pueblo Style, evolved up to the American army occupation in 1846. American influence and efforts to cope with erosion resulted in the later and currently popular Territorial Adobe Style. About 1833 approximately one-hundred fifty Mexicans from Fernando de Taos, Nueve Mejico, were hired and traveled north to build Bent's Old Fort, for they were familiar with the techniques involved in adobe construction.

Adobe is comparable to concrete. When adobe was made, one part clay was mixed with three parts sand and four percent

---

[5] Neil M. Judd, *The Use of Adobe in Prehistoric Dwellings of the Southwest* (Washington, D.C.: Government Printing Office, 1916). The major advantage of adobe structures is their thick walls — for protection, for personal comfort, etc. The major disadvantage of adobe buildings is that the natural material erodes.

water was added (the less water used the stronger it is). If too much clay was used, the adobe would be initially strong but then would shrink, warp, and crack. Conversely, if too much sand was used, the adobe would be weak and crumble. Straw was not a reinforcement, as was popularly believed, but created small air passages for more even curing and greater strength.The straw, added to the mud plaster, diverted the water and reduced the surface erosion. The alternative of Mexican wool was mentioned by George Grinnell, but no specific evidence was found of its use in the case of Bent's Old Fort.

In conjunction with the historic architectural research, tests were made in the laboratory to determine the composition of the original adobe and to analyze the raw materials within the vicinity of the fort site. The laboratory tests determined that the original adobes consisted mostly of silt rather than clay. Silt has little strength and explains the rapid disintegration of the original adobe. Utilizing the laboratory data, sample adobe bricks were manufactured in the field in order to develop the right combination of the ingredients for maximum strength, durability, and historic authenticity for the reconstruction of the fort. Stabilized adobe bricks, those that have admixtures of either chemical compounds, asphalt, or soil cement for more strength and less erosion, were also manufactured and analyzed. The architects who were visited in Taos and Santa Fe advised on the adobe construction techniques — from the original authentic hand method to the many types of machine manufactured adobe. The research on adobe construction, both historic and modern, was completed in the late summer of 1973.[6]

Although the historical evidence revealed no specific time-table, conjecture, based on architectural logic as well as ar-chaeological clues, suggested that the fort was constructed in the following phases:

1. north gate, north rooms on the west side, northeast bastion, east, south, and west rooms — all forming a square around the plaza,

2. east and south corral walls and southwest bastion, with a simple wagon shed on the south open on the north side,

---

[6] The minimum acceptable properties of the adobe were: compression — 400 pounds-per-square-inch (PSI) for natural and 1,000 PSI for stabilized; moisture — 4 percent by weight; absorption — 20 percent at seven days on one face; rupture shear — 40-50 PSI; erosion — 1/16 inch at two hours of 20 PSI water spray; freeze-thaw-nonsprawling.

3. north trade rooms on the east,

4. second-floor quarters on the west, St. Vrain's room, north guard house and belfry, and the billiard room,

5. wagon shed replaced by permanent storage area for the military supplies and a new wagon shed to the south in the new larger corral.

It seemed clear that historically the fort was remodeled and expanded frequently, a relatively easy procedure with adobe construction. For example, William Boggs refers in 1844 to a blacksmith shop in the northwest corner, and the archaeologists found evidence of this. There was also evidence that the area used earlier as a back gate at the center of the south plaza became the present blacksmith shop when the back wagon house and corrals were added.

With the major guidelines for reconstruction essentially established, the process of making the architectural drawings began. The design drawings were made freehand, by Thorson, to illustrate the handmade nature of the adobe construction. Drawn to scale on a grid instead of written dimensions, they detailed the historic as well as the contemporary aspects of the structure. During this process many architectural items were refined, and the entire plan became more fully integrated.

The next stage was to evaluate the research data to make the design decisions. In architecture there are always four factors to be balanced: function, aesthetics, techniques (engineering and maintenance), and finances. In historic preservation the aesthetic (or historic) factor, the prime reason for the project, has the main emphasis. The evaluation and design procedure was based first on analyzing the facts — the on-site archaeology and historical evidence, particularly Lieutenant Abert's drawings and diary. Second, logic and conjecture were applied to hypothecate how a typical function or detail might have been executed by the Taos Mexicans and Indians, as directed by the Anglos from the East. In a sense the continuing problem was to get inside the mind of William Bent, who master-minded the original construction. Third, modifications for safety, engineering, and maintenance — concessions to modern technology — were defined. Finally, and fortunately, funding did not turn out to be a major problem, although economical use of the public funds was a constant injunction.

Most of the roof types and the dimensions were determined by the historical data, particularly Lieutenant Abert's drawings. However, the dimensions of the billiard room and the pantry were based on typical pueblo architecture. The framing plan, showing vigas and posts, was based primarily on the archaeological ruins, which indicated the direction of the beams along with the typical framing of that period. The vigas would vary from 8 inches to 12 inches in diameter, depending on the span, and an average 2 feet 8 inches on center. The spacing would also vary, showing extra posts for support of sagging beams and other natural imperfections.

In the Abert elevations of the court, round vigas were drawn. However, the Abert watercolor of the council room showed rectangular beams with a plank ceiling. Therefore, three rooms (108, 109, and 110) have rectangular beams. A concern was to maintain correct scale of members, although the loads for visitors would be greater today than they were originally.

Entry 100 was formed by the two pair of gates. It had a hatch opening into the trade room (101) and was occasionally used by the Indians for trade.

Above the main entrance, the watch tower (201) had small windows on three sides and a door on the south. The primary source for the dimensions was the Abert sketch. The belfry above was open and housed the eagles and the bell; and the flag pole was on the west side (Abert). Neither the bell nor any historical information regarding it was found, so its inclusion was based upon conjecture.

Three trade rooms (101, 102, and 103) were similar, with connecting doors and raised sills, back-to-back American fireplaces in rooms 101 and 102, and a semicorner Indian fireplace in room 103. According to the archaeological data, the vigas in 103 spanned east-west (opposite of normal framing) and projected on the east. This indicated that this room may have been built earlier, along with the east rooms.

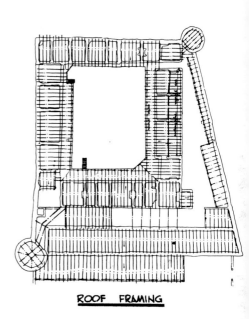

ROOF FRAMING

These rooms will be a visitors' reception-sales area and for audio-visual presentations. Therefore, additional electrified candle fixtures are shown.

Bastion 104, one of the unique round towers, was framed diagonally with many posts, determined by the archaeological data, to support a swivel cannon on the upper floor. The ladder was included on the side (Abert). The trench going under the wall may have been some form of drainage or privy. The "coal hole" is a mystery; it will be shown only with ghost image where it was filled in later.

An alley (105) led from the plaza to corral 106, which was the original stockade for all the animals, but later, after the corral to the south was built, it was presumably used only for special animals.

Battlement 204, one of the outside walls, was the firing line of the fortress. The parapet was 4 feet high, enough to protect a defender or enable him to be fired over. The portholes for musket fire were shown three different ways in the historical data — conical, horizontal, and vertical. Abert provided the most complete description, probably due to his military background. The architects' consensus was that they were vertical, about 6 inches wide by 8 inches high on the outside, and sloping inside to approximately 14 inches by 14 inches at a 30-inch height for firing from a kneeling position.

Abert's drawings of the court show all of the roofs of the east rooms sloping inward toward the plaza, and there were no handrails or parapets on the plaza side. This was where Indians and other people of the fort sat to watch functions in the plaza. However, one of the Abert drawings shows a possible parapet on the exterior side of these east rooms. For this as well as safety reasons, a 2-foot parapet is shown along the east side and around the south to the billiard room, the presumed original exterior walls.

Council room 108 was a major area, used as a council room with the Indians, a living room, and a visitor's quarters.

FORT BENT
DRAWN FROM ORIGINAL SKETCHES
BY LIEUT. J.W. ABERT 1845-46

The rectangular beams had two intermediate beams supported from adobe buttresses and posts, due to the bigger span. The American style fireplace along the north wall could have had the shepherd's shelf above it, typical of New Mexican style.

In trade room 109 special trading was probably carried on in firearms, gun powder, jewelry, and other articles. There was on-site evidence of the counter, the shelves, and the pit cellar.

The dining room (110), the largest room in the fort, was a center of social activity. The mid-span beams were supported by three posts in the center of the room. Surprisingly, no fireplace was indicated, but heat was obviously provided, probably from an oven or brazier in the center of the room. The historical record refers to "winding stairs going up to St. Vrain's room above," and a base and a sill for stairs was found on the site in the northwest corner. A true spiral stairs is, of course, not in evidence and if there was one it could not have ascended to St. Vrain's quarters, which were above the cook's room. Therefore, a stairs rising to a landing, offset, and then going to St. Vrain's is conjectured.

The cook's room (111) was the serving area, possibly Charlotte Green's room, and furnishings indicated that it was also utilized by many children at the fort. It would have had a connecting door for serving.

The kitchen (112) had the largest fireplace and stone hearth in the fort, determined by the archaeological data. Although trappers and other workers probably cooked in their own quarters, the meals for principals of the fort and honored guests were prepared here.

The pantry (113), a small room off the kitchen, probably added later, had a fairly well-preserved adobe foundation in the cellar, which was down 4½ feet. (This wall was expected to be an in-situ remains exhibit.) Steps and shelves completed this room.

Although there was no archaeological evidence due to ground disturbances, hornos, adobe beehive ovens used for baking, were located outside to

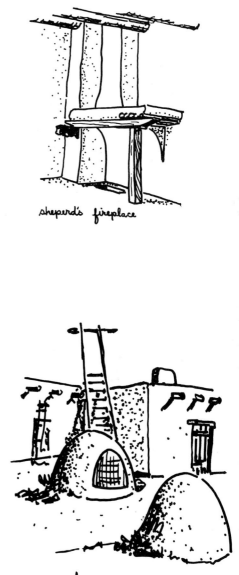

sheperd's fireplace

hornos

portal

keep the heat out in the summer. Two are drawn in the area near the kitchen.

The stables (107 and 137), two shed areas in the inner corral, were similar with a wood portal roof. Stable 107 was probably more of a shelter for animals, used to separate them from one another.

The Bents' quarters (115 and 116) were two rooms that formed a suite for William Bent with sleeping area, living room, and office. The niche in 115 was presumably a closet.

Four work rooms (117, 118, 119, and 120), designated by supposed function and positioned as remembered by George Bent, would have had connecting doors and American fireplaces. Two sources mentioned the blacksmith shop (118) with a forge located in the southwest corner. Five sources mentioned the carpenter's shop (120), and a gunsmith shop (119) and wheelright (117) were also indicated.

The alley corral (139), an open area, had widely-spaced vigas and a woodbrush roof, forming a sun shelter much like the ramada of Taos Pueblo.

The wagon house (122-34) probably was open on the north side, when it housed the twelve to fifteen large wagons mentioned in the historical sources. However, when the expansion occurred and the wagon shed was relocated in the new corral, this area was built higher with a roof at 12 feet and was probably used for military supplies, a fact that might not have been advertised. The Abert drawing shows steps from the porch of the billiard room up 2 feet to the roof. (This is the administrative area.)

The wagon shed (136), a wood-roofed structure, will conceal the few automobiles permitted to drive to the fort, as well as the electrical transformer. The barn doors to the administrative general office (133) have personnel doors for access and safety exit.

The main corral at the rear of the fort (137) was enclosed by a 6-foot-high wall topped with prickly pear cactus to discourage raiders.

The billiard room (211) was a unique room that bridged from the main fort across the alley to the wagon house. On the east there was a porch with a portal above and the entrance door. Handrails were added for safety, although no supportive evidence was found. The fireplace and a small bar were at the west end on Abert's sketch.

Bastion 135, the larger bastion, was 27 feet in diameter and similar to the northeast bastion, except for a center opening for a main ladder and stronger support of posts. An exit door is included for safety and functional use, although no evidence for or against it was found. A bridge and stairs connects the upper level to the second floor.

Room (141) was a small area that presented a mystery, although possible use as a smoke house or for gun powder storage was suggested by the historians. Logical use was as a powder room because the room was isolated and located near cistern water.

Presumably the principals used chamber pots in their rooms; however, other residents apparently used the privy (143) when the cold or dangers prevented them from going outside the fort. There was a trench along the west wall, and it was near the cistern for water. It may have been combined with the adjacent wash area.

The stairs going down to a two-level pit in one of the storage rooms (145) were an interesting problem, as they started outside of the only door, which would make the main level floor inaccessible. It was concluded that a wood plank floor existed over the pit with a trap door at the entrance, much like a farm cellar. This room was referred to by Francis Parkman: "so producing a rusty key, he opened a low door which led to a half-subterranean apartment, into which the two disappeared together," and the archaeological data revealed the log framing support for the floor. Another storage room (146) had a round pit about 3 feet deep, which was never explained. Conjecture offers the possibilities of either a "cock pit" or some special storage.

A sunken well (147), sheathed with wood plank walls, had stairs leading

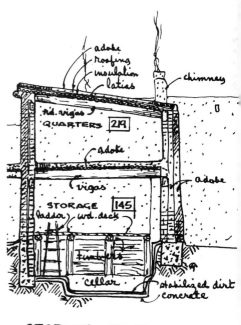

STORAGE ROOM

corner fireplace.

down from inside the room. Archaeological and historical evidence indicates the existence of three wells but only one at a single time, this being the one of 1846. A later well was found at the council room.

An area that was probably the main quarters for the Mexican workers and trappers (148-51) was noted by the Spanish-type corner fireplaces. These may have had other uses occasionally, as indicated by Boggs and George Bent. Susan Magoffin mentioned Indian women in the room below hers. Two rooms (148 and 149) are adaptively used for interpretive staff quarters.

Not too much is known about quarters (217-22) as there was no on-site evidence. However, the clerk's room (217) apparently had a short bridge to the door, shown by Abert. This plan also shows chimneys in several of the rooms (217, 218, 220, and 222) for corner fireplaces. The end room (222) had to be the one mentioned by Susan Magoffin in her diary because of the two windows looking out on the plaza and the river.

St. Vrain's quarters (207) was another special guest room with a corner fireplace. The door and portal are on the west side, as drawn by Abert.

In addition to the many rooms of the fort, special details indicate an important part of the architectural challenge of authentic reconstruction.

As mentioned previously, primarily two main styles of fireplaces existed, although there were variations of each. The corner fireplaces were of the Mexican and Indian type, where the fire was built in tepee fashion. The cheeked fireplaces along the wall were of American design, and often two were backed up to each other in an H shape.

The chimneys were high adobe stacks; however, if they did not draw they were extended by stacking open pots on top. The final designs were, of necessity, based on some degree of conjecture.

Two external stairs run from the second floor down to the plaza. They were wood and had rough handrails for safety. Other ladders of the Indian type ran from the first to the second floor and on to the roofs. Some of these are in evidence on Abert's drawing, and others were located where it was deemed logical.

Rain gutter spouts or canales projected about 2 feet through the adobe parapets and were located on the lower side of the roofs. The taper of the roof vigas was set in the same direction to provide the natural slope for drainage. These were located according to need and logic.

canale

The doors and the gates were sometimes evidenced in the ruins, but not always, as there may have been a buried adobe sill or a step-over curb. Therefore, historical evidence or conjecture of an absolute need was used.

The main north gate, shown by Abert as 6½ feet by 7 feet high, was extremely small for wagons to enter. Historical sources also indicated "a pair of immense plank doors" and a "massive gate." The ruins indicated about an 8-foot opening with evidence of posts. Therefore, the architects showed the larger opening with a pair of wood planked doors sheathed with metal and nail studs and swinging in, as described by the historical sources. There also was a similar pair of gates on the inside, forming a protected entry area or Zaguan. The east corral gates were of the same construction, as determined by historical and archaeological research. Although not confirmed, the south corral would have one larger gate, more like a regular cattle gate with vertical log pickets. From the south corral through the wagon house, although the ruins were destroyed in this area by a later road, there must have been barn doors to connect the two corrals. Historical evidence indicated a cattle gate near the pantry and stable, controlling the alley.

doors

The plaza door openings are apparent on Abert's drawings, although they were too high to show on the archaeological data. Because no doors were visible in the sketch, it was speculated whether or not they existed. However, Abert mentions that an Indian named Ah-Mah-Nah-Co "knocked at the door of my room" and posed for a sketch, the same one pictured on the reverse of the fort drawings. Studies indicated connecting doors with raised sills joining the council room (108), a trade room (109), and the dining room (110). There also would have been a connecting door to the cook's room (111) for serving rather than taking food outside. Similar connecting doors are shown near the blacksmith shop (118). At this room the archaeological data showed a major opening with an outside plank floor. This was probably the back gate referred to by Boggs and would be required for the blacksmith. Studies indicated an unusual arched opening.

Plaza windows were also drawn by Abert. Other windows were above the level of the ruins, so not confirmed by archaeology. However, based on conjective, four types were drawn: Crown glass, barred with interior wood shutters, oiled animal skin, and translucent selenite stone. The final selections were based on typical pueblo architecture. A major premise was that a fort would not have exterior windows, so, based on phased construction, it was assumed that there were no windows on the east side of the rooms (109-114) to the inner corral.

Despite the lack of historical evidence, handrails were added for safety to stairs and to the bridges to the bastions. However, Abert's drawings clearly show no handrails at the roof edge to the plaza, so these were not added as they would be definite historical intrusions. Any railing along the edge of the portal would also have ruined the building from a photographic standpoint. A portable rope rail may be required for safety, but this will not confuse the visitor as to historical accuracy.

There is no reference to a chapel or other evidence of religious practices in the historical data. The Mexicans were generally Roman Catholic, while the Bents were Protestant. There probably was a small niche for a shrine in the Mexican area and perhaps a cross hanging on the wall.

window shutters

With the basic design decisions established, the construction drawings were made, utilizing the historical, archaeological, and architectural research. The numerous drawings that covered the structural, the electrical, and the mechanical details illustrated the union of all of the research and the creative ingenuity of the planners. The original fort did not have a foundation, for the builders simply started by digging a slight trench and laying adobes; however, a reinforced mass concrete foundation, three feet deep was programed and drawn for the reconstruction. Thus, the floor would be authentic adobe mud over a concrete slab, and the adobe floor would be given an oil and turpentine finish for sealing and hardening. The walls were to consist of stabilized adobe for the structural bearing core and natural adobe for the exterior. The stabilized adobe plaster

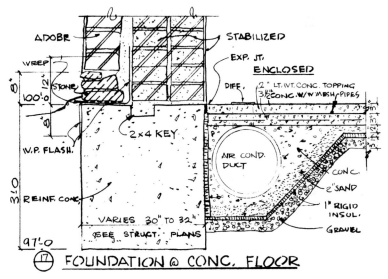

would be apparent on the interior, but the plaster on the exterior would erode naturally and would be patched annually in the historic tradition.[7] The ceilings and the roofs were drawn as a composite system, with vigas set in a concrete bond beam, supporting latias, straw, insulation, three-inch concrete, roofing membrane, and topped with three inches of adobe and gravel. The appearance of the roof would be similar to the approximate

[7] The exterior plaster is natural adobe mud, very stable when dry. But rain will result in deep erosion ruts on the west wall. Historically, the same situation would have occurred. A stone ledge with scuppers was hollowed out, half-log vertical troughs were added, but annual exterior adobe patching will be required.

eight inches of adobe of the original, but the roof would be stronger and more weatherproof. Radiant pipes were to be included in the ceilings where another room was to be superimposed.

Among the numerous drawings, the mechanical and the electrical drawings covering the modern-day conveniences presented interesting challenges. In order to have a concealed heat source in the historical areas, the heating plan was drawn as a low temperature, hot water, radiant pipe system within the adobe floor. Temperatures in the historic areas were designed to be sixty degrees Farenheit in order to have less differentiation with the outside in the interest of authenticity. Twenty-two different fireplaces were designed not only for their historical accuracy but also for their functions to augment the heating source. Only the staff area was programed for an air conditioning system in the floor, and this area was also designated for all of the mechanical equipment, the staff restroom, shower, kitchenette, and the public comfort station.

The electrical drawings showed the lighting, power, and special systems. A minimum of one electrified candle per historic room was designed, with the switches controlled from an electrical panel that would not be visible in the room. The candles would be housed in authentically fabricated fixtures with wiring for fifteen watts. The historical areas would be provided with one outlet per room, concealed by the furnishings. However, in the staff area the lighting and the power were to be conventional, using compatible modern Spanish-type lights. The fire detection and the alarm systems were to be recessed into the ceiling latias, and the burglar system would be concealed as well. In order to portray the unique nature of this historic construction, some imperfections and signs of repair that would have been made by the original adobe makers from Taos were to be apparent.

Construction funds were received in January 1975, and procedures for contracting were initiated. Due to the special nature of constructing adobe historically, it was decided to negotiate a cost-plus-fixed-fee contract. Studies have revealed that this contract is advantageous to the government, for the contractor is reimbursed for actual costs and has a guaranteed fee, which encourages him to perform quality work and save money. This method, though it required closer supervision and cost account monitoring, gave the NPS specialists the opportunity to have direct participation in evaluating the construction process.

Just prior to the public announcement of funding, the Small Business Administration requested a section 8A "set-aside" for a Spanish-American contractor, the firm of Mershon and Gimeno of Denver. The NPS agreed to investigate the qualifications of the firm and to negotiate costs to determine if these were acceptable to the government. Emil Gimeno evidenced considerable knowledge for this type of a construction project, was enthusiastic about western history, and was personally dedicated to furthering the cause of the Spanish-American workers. The firm's cost estimate was within the governmental estimate, and their fixed fee was reasonable. So they were awarded the contract which, in the final accounting, came to $1,350,000.

Russ Jones, the contractor's superintendent (not to be confused with architect T. Russell Jones of the NPS), was an experienced masonry foreman who had taught masons in Denver, a useful talent for training the adobe-layers at the fort. Tilio Romero, lead carpenter and mason, arrived from Taos along with other workers who were experienced at working with adobe and historic wood tools — as used in the original construction.

Robert Smith of the Denver Service Center was assigned as project supervisor. His preceding project, the restoration of Castle Clinton, a masonry fortification of 1812 in New York City, was markedly different from the adobe of the Southwest but both were historical, and he had a longstanding interest in adobe construction and had made studies on the fort in the 1960s. Thorson and exhibit specialist Thomas Armstrong provided technical consultation for the Denver office, and with fellow architect Jones made frequent inspection trips, continuing the research on architectural details.

The actual reconstruction of Bent's Old Fort began on 28 May 1975. And while the construction progressed, research was completed, refinements were made, and changes were incorporated, based on information gathered during the construction process. The cost-plus-fixed-fee contract provided this flexibility to improve continually the techniques and the materials, ensuring the best possible final product.[8]

[8] Just prior to starting the construction of the fort a purchase order (for $9,750) was issued to capture the construction process on film. The film team from the Department of Communications at the University of Denver was headed by Dr. Richard Foushee, a historian and visiting professor teaching film production. He and his film crew traveled to the fort frequently to film the work and to capture the sounds of construction. In the fall of 1975, competitive proposals were received to complete the filming, develop the script, and edit the final twenty-six minute documentary film. The committee selected Eugene-Claire Productions with the same film team. The total cost was approximately $35,000, and the film tells the architectural story for the general public and is available for schools, meetings, and television.

The construction drawings, incorporating the precise structural data revealed by archaeology, provided the basis for laying out the grid and the foundation measurements. Excavation was done under the close observation of archaeologist Robert Leonard of Colorado State University. This paid off, for previously unknown historical remains were found at the east wall near the the well. The contractor worked around this area while the archaeologist and his crew uncovered their find. This revealed stairs running down from the room about three steps under the wall and then continuing outside to a depth of about seven feet, leading into a room of about twenty by sixteen feet. This subterranean feature, which could be either pre- or post-Bent period, was refilled with sand for protection, and studies proceeded on dating and identification. Meanwhile, the two previously designated in-situ adobe remnants proved to be too fragile to save, but another remnant in the northeast trade room was found and was preserved behind glass as an in-situ exhibit.

After excavation, the foundations were lined with ninety pound roofing felt, instead of wood forms, because this would better conform to the irregular line of the wall. The workers, accustomed to straight foundations, at first thought a mistake had been made and had to be reassured. The historic wall alignment, based on archaeological data, represented the original freehand construction technique. (The original alignment had additional irregularities resulting from over a century of erosion and patching.) Far from offending the eye, this technique reflected the true sculptural beauty of handcrafted adobe. The concrete foundation pour was the biggest in Otero County; mixer trucks had to be brought over from Pueblo to assist.

The adobe manufacturer for the stabilized core of the adobe walls was Admode of Canon City. Made in a rammed earth block machine, each unit was compressed from a poured 8 inches to the required 4 inches. As a minimum of water for forming and a 10 percent cement additive was used, the resultant block tested at 2,000 pounds-per-square inch, twice the required specifications and as strong as concrete block. The color and shape were acceptable and the cost was reasonable.

The natural adobe required for surfacing was more difficult to locate, as this had to be completely authentic in appearance and preferably of a local source to facilitate future repairs. Three local adobe makers offered to make these by standard hand methods, but their products could not meet the quality or quantity required. Several experiments failed, but finally Reed and Son of La Junta developed an efficient technique for the mass manufacture of adobe bricks. The soil in the immediate vicinity of the fort proved to be unusable because of a preponderance of silt; however, soil with the good proportions of clay and sand was found elsewhere in the area of La Junta.[9]

Finally the adobe laying began. Adobe work requires special skills, different from those used by regular brick masons. It

The laying of the adobe bricks required special skills, skills that differed some from those of a skilled mason. The adobes were laid in combinations, using mortar that was basically of the same mix as the adobe but with smaller sand particles. All of the wall was tied into one mass—resulting in a "monolithic wall." The regular maintenance of the adobe and the interpretive program would be combined. Repairing the mud plaster on the exterior adobe wall would be done in the historic method as a learning experience for visitors.

[9] If adobes are made from river soil, they are generally weak; but if made from soil taken from higher ground, where the erosion marks are vertical, they are stronger. Lab tests were made, but a real adobe maker can tell good adobe by feel and taste. Reed and Son developed a machine to make adobes that facilitated the production process.

seemed easier to train a new person than to retrain a skilled mason. Accordingly, the adobes were layed by trained Spanish-Americans from Taos and some local, untrained people from La Junta.

Instead of buttering the top and the edge of each unit, as with standard fired brick, adobes are laid in combinations. A whole row of adobes is first laid on a mud bed and the joints and the cavities are then filled; the result is a monolithic wall. Reinforcing ties are placed in the joints at regular intervals to increase the bond between the stabilized core and the natural type adobes. Adobe fireplaces are layed up in rectangular units, then the rounded openings are cut and plastered with mud.

Meanwhile, the search for suitable timbers for the interior structural framework continued. The samples of wood retrieved archaeologically were sent to the Colorado State University laboratory at Fort Collins for identification. These samples were found to be cottonwood and pine, confirming architectural assumptions. Cottonwood, available near the fort, was used first in the original construction. But, as the supply of these trees dwindled, and the builders discovered how cottonwood warped, they must have moved upstream to the foothills of the Rocky Mountains and floated pine down to the fort. A supply of straight cottonwood on private property was found sheltered along the river west of Pueblo, near the site of Bent's first stockade, and a purchase agreement was made. Then the task of timbering and hauling to the fort began. After an additional search, including an Indian reservation in New Mexico, pine was purchased, timbered, and brought in from a locality north of Denver. The timbers were dried at the site in the hot summer air, some Indian tepee style and others cross-stacked. The bark

was stripped with draw knives, which is easier to do when the wood is either green or thoroughly cured.

After curing, the wood was fashioned into vigas (support beams), doors, windows, and stairs. Tilio Romero, Daniel Medina, and John Romero were the nucleus of the carpentry crew. Because it is critical in historic preservation projects to have correct tool marks on the final finished surface, a modern tool like a chain saw can be used for rough work to speed up the process, but a genuine historic tool must be used for finishing. So the viga ends that projected were pointed with an axe.

Armstrong arrived in Denver about this time and added his historical construction experience to the project. Research showed a hand adze was used on much of the work done on doors, frames, and windows. One of the workers remembered some old tools that were abandoned behind his uncle's barn in Taos, and turned up with two adzes that were serviceable with rust removed and new handles added. Armstrong found other adzes in antique stores in Denver. Different people use the tool differently, some straddle the log and other stand side-saddle. The two techniques result in slightly different angles to the chipping marks. A mechanical adze, used previously in Yorktown, Virginia, was tried, but it was a cutting head on a high speed router, and the results were too uniform for handwork.

For the large rectangular roof members on the east side, it was determined that a broad axe should be employed, as it was quicker and easier for big areas. A block plane was used sometimes to dress-up the more finished work. A chain saw effectively cut out a big notch for stairs; this was followed by a chisel;

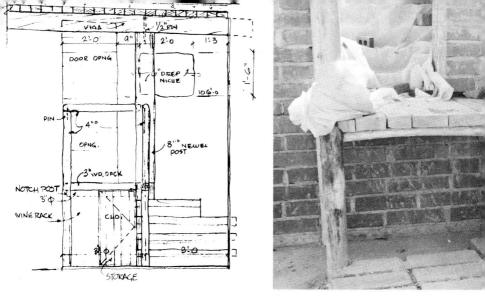

For authenticity, no modern tool marks were left exposed on the finished adobe outpost. Like the entire fort, the solid cottonwood stairway from the dining room to St. Vrain's quarters advanced

but no rotary saw marks or other modern tool marks were exposed. Winding stairs from the dining room to St. Vrain's quarters were made from solid pieces of cottonwood, with simulated wear on the treads.

The cottonwood and the pine pieces were not intermingled indiscriminately. Rather, they were used in two distinctly different sections of the fort, according to the respective stage of architectural evolution. In substance, it was hypothecated that the newer section of the fort was the northeast quadrant, which included the trade room on the north side of the east entrance and the council room and dining room along the east wall. It was here, therefore, that the pine predominated. The balance of the older section of the fort and most of the vertical support posts and horizontal beams or vigas were predominantly cottonwood.

Interior adobe plaster against the adobe had to be stabilized or reinforced, so research samples were tried with varying amounts of cement, lime, special chemicals, and natural adobe. Surprisingly, pure natural adobe gave the hardest, most stable surface as long as it was kept dry. As expected, multiple, not too moist layers, resulted in the least shrinkage and cracks. Next came the question of the plaster wall colors. Archaeological samples were checked and three distinct color tones emerged — a dull earth red, a brownish yellow ochre, and a smoky white. The pigment would have been an organic, natural material. It was determined that it would have been applied by hand, using a sheep skin. However, these were duplicated for modern pur-

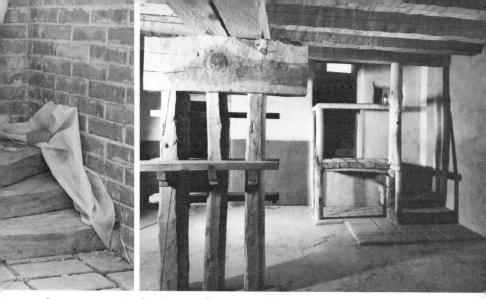

from construction drawings to the completed stairway, employing a variety of building and finishing techniques.

poses by experimenting with commercial dry pigments in a water base, applied with a rough burlap dauber. A refinement suggested by an archaeological fragment and the example of the historic Governor's Palace at Santa Fe was the additional use — in the dining room, clerk's room, and William Bent's bedroom — of a red fabric wainscoting. This fabric, originally a fine muslin but now polyester, was applied with glue.

The exterior coating of natural adobe mud, quite stable when dry, can be readily reapplied after erosion by weathering. No wire mesh was used to ensure adhesion, except at concrete beam bondings and roof flashings. The general use of netting was proscribed because it would be an artificial element when exposed by weathering. To minimize erosion from rain, wooden gutter spouts or canales project about two feet through the adobe parapets, on the down sides of the roofs. The viga taper was outward to ensure a natural slope for drainage. When unusually heavy rainfall during the construction resulted in some rapid erosion, stone ledges with scuppers and vertical half-log troughs or downspouts were added.

While the design and the construction of the basic structure of the facade and interior walls posed problems, these were not as acute as those related to the various structural details where documentary and archaeological data were less helpful, and the architect had to place more reliance on educated conjecture.

The original floors were simply earth or clay packed by usage. (Susan Magoffin noted in 1846 that a mixture of water and oil was sprinkled on the floors to keep down the dust.) To prepare these for trampling by thousands of visitors, samples were tried using different mixes and amounts of water. The moist, soupy mix had big shrinkage cracks, but the dry pack mix that was tamped in resulted in a surface "hard as concrete."

Native sandstone suitable for foundations and hearths was located in a nearby quarry. While no historical evidence was found for a parapet railing around the edge of the plaza, in the interest of safety a low stone barrier was placed here. Coated with adobe this does not do violence to the integrity of the appearance of the plaza.

Sketches of architectural hardware were made based on the artifacts uncovered at the site as well as comparative Southwest types. The blacksmiths at the fort designed modifications to fit specific requirements. A concealed metal sleeve with ball bearings was added to the heavy entrance door pivot pins for opening ease. The exterior stockade gates of sharpened vertical poles with cross-braces requiring maximum stoutness were not changed. The interior stockade gates were designed with an open "Z" brace. The barn-type doors for access into the staff area were restudied. Although the prototype in Taos had swung in, most swing out, so the hardware was redesigned accordingly. The lag bolts for hardware and rails had their heads hand-worked by the blacksmith.

As to finishing the wood, the historical architects had first to determine the appearance of the wood after a period of about fifteen years. So additional field explorations of earlier adobe structures in southern Colorado and northern New Mexico were made and methods of antiquing wood were researched. It was understood that exterior wood aged differently than interior wood due to the effects of water and sun. The interior cottonwood, starting with a natural yellow appearance, would gradually change to a tan and eventually to a brown. In addition, smoke would have a blackening effect around the fireplace, up the adobe walls, and on the ceiling, more so on the top side of the vigas where it would settle. The exterior wood would weather grey, a lighter shade with touches of tan when in the shade or protected from water, a darker shade when exposed to more water or sun, such as on the projecting vigas near the adobe wall and on the south side.

Experiments were conducted using Cabots' bleaching oil and bleaching stains, but they all had an objectionable sheen. Naturally aged wood has a very flat, dull appearance and when

On the left the doors open into the council room, the dining room, and the cook's quarters with St. Vrain's room on the second level. The projecting vigas and the drying furs add to the plaza scene.

exposed to weather tends to show grooves and hollows. After futile experiments with water, pigments were mixed with alcohol as a vehicle. The result was convincing. Next, it was decided to sandblast lightly or wire brush to erode the softer material on the exterior wood, followed by a bristle brush to enhance an aged appearance.

Historical modes of illumination offered an excellent opportunity to inject some fine detail into the structure. Candle holders were fabricated in the fort's blacksmith shop, the designs based on the furnishings studies and comparative data of southwestern fixtures. They included glass-paned lanterns, pierced-tin lanterns, hogscrapers with piston risers, simple candle holders, wall sconces, and various chandeliers. Some were hung from ropes through pulleys at the ceiling for the replacing of candles. An original brass bulls-eye lantern, known to be in use at the fort, also had to be reproduced. All known candle flame bulbs were investigated — flicker flames, incandescent flame bulbs, neon flame, etc. — but none had a sufficient flame-like appearance. A Swedish manufactured flame bulb sold by Cima of New York was found. It is a small bulb, the same size and color as a candle flame, on a pendulum and spring

The re-created blacksmith's shop at the fort was used to fabricate the candle holders and other metal fixtures.

inside a plastic candle. An electromagnet is actuated on a 30-to-60-second cycle, causing the bulb to wave like a real flame. Its 3 watts provides a similar illumination and its 2,000-hour life was practical. The plastic candles were to be coated to look like real buffalo tallow candles.

In addition to the reconstruction of the fort itself, the master plan provided for certain public facilities. The original plan as of 1966 had called for a maintenance building, staff housing, and a visitor center along the north boundary, but subsequent planning eliminated all outside structures except for the maintenance building. All visitor facilities were incorporated inside the fort; thus, the view from the fort parapets would not be spoiled by intrusive modern structures. (The maintenance building in the far northwestern corner of the area will be camouflaged by trees.)

Other site developmental features included the entrance gate, the entrance road, the parking area, and the walkway to the fort.[10] The parking area is located in a slight draw about four hundred yards from the fort. The walkway is rough-surfaced and follows the original Santa Fe Trail along the first bench above the river bottom. The intent of the planners was to simu-

[10] The site developmental features were under a separate contract with the architects/engineers of the URS/Ken R. White Company. The site project was bid and let to the Carlson Construction Company in February 1976 and was completed that summer.

late the experience of trail travelers approaching the fort, giving modern visitors exposed sun, wind, and rain — a mild foretaste of frontier hardships, the better to appreciate the primitive quality of the fort. (The NPS will supply special wheel transportation for the aged, the handicapped, or others for whom the journey from parking lot to reconstructed fort would be too much of a hardship.)

Among the structures associated with the era of geographical exploration and the fur trade, Bent's Old Fort ranks as one of four great trading posts that were bastions in the wilderness, all of which are now historic sites in the national park system. Log-stockaded Fort Vancouver in Oregon territory, built by the Hudson's Bay Company and a focal point of the American occupation of Oregon, will be only partially reconstructed. The site of the adobe-walled Fort Laramie in Wyoming, which became a major military post on the Oregon Trail, has been preempted by later military structures, and will never be rebuilt. All that is left of mighty Fort Union of the American Fur Company on the Upper Missouri are archaeological remains, and prospects for its reconstruction are dim. Among these four outposts of empire, only Bent's Old Fort has been fully reconstructed — to give modern visitors a keener perception of the value and meaning of their unique American frontier heritage.[11]

GEORGE A. THORSON was director of design for the URS/Ken R. White Company and project architect for the reconstruction of Bent's Old Fort. A graduate of the University of Illinois and a practicing architect for twenty-seven years in Colorado, he has been architect for a number of historic buildings in the state and is now serving on the American Institute of Architects National Committee for Historic Resources. He edited ARCHITECTURE COLORADO: MOUNTAINS, MINES, AND MANSIONS, and currently he is senior historical architect in the historic preservation branch at the National Park Service.

[11] In December 1976 the Award of the Colorado Society of the American Institute of Architects was presented to the URS Company, A&E Consultants, and George A. Thorson. In addition, the National Park Service as client and the Mershon Gimeno Construction Company as contractor were honored. The special design award was given "in recognition of effort and time devoted in preservation of our architectural heritage" (John W. Henneberger, Denver Service Center, to Regional Director, Rocky Mountain Region, P4417-DSC-MH).

Furnishing a Frontier Outpost

BY SARAH M. OLSON

The process of furnishing Bent's Old Fort basically consisted of three broad steps, and it was begun in conjunction with the architectural study in 1973. The first step was the preparation of a "Furnishing Study" that recorded all of the available documentation of the fort's furnishings. This study was completed in August 1974 and was followed by a "Furnishing Plan" that provided a room-by-room blueprint for the acquisition and the installation of the furnishings. In 1976 the long process of acquisition and installation commenced and essentially was completed by the summer of 1977.[1]

Prior to embarking upon the "Furnishing Study," the historic date that would be used to depict the fort was decided by a mutual agreement between historians and architects of the National Park Service. While the history of Bent's Old Fort spanned only sixteen years, its structure and functions evolved to the extent that a re-creation of the fort in the 1830s would have differed markedly in appearance from the fort of the 1840s. The few available descriptions, both exterior and interior, were mainly by-products of the brief presence in 1846 of the Army of the West and its unsung chroniclers. Therefore, the furnishings, as well as the architecture, necessarily had to reflect this best known period. It was decided, however, that the furnishings should maintain the primary trading post function that normally characterized the fort rather than its brief military occupation.

With the 1846 date established, all of the primary source material for information regarding functions of rooms, items of furniture, and activities that suggested the presence of particular objects or types of objects was reviewed. Such primary sources included the results of archaeological surveys, the trade books of Bent, St. Vrain & Company, and the accounts of various travelers.

The most valuable evidence of the furnishings at the fort was contained in the findings of the archaeological survey carried on at the site by the National Park Service between 1963 and 1966.[2] The functions of many of the rooms were established by this survey along with the identification of several classes of

These brass, dragon- or serpent-shaped side plates are from Northwest or Hudson's Bay guns unearthed at the site.

objects present at the fort during the 1830s and 1840s. Some of these latter finds were surprising. For instance, while the presence of the Northwest trade gun was anticipated, the survey uncovered unexpected evidence of traffic in the full-stocked Deringer Indian trade rifle.

In some cases, the archaeological findings not only confirmed but clarified what had heretofore been only vague references from nineteenth-century travelers. For example, during the period from 1845 to 1847 travelers' observations confirmed a fur press in the center of the plaza,[3] and part of the press appeared in Lieutenant James W. Abert's watercolor of an 1845 scalp dance held in the plaza of the fort. The exact location of the press and the fact that it was of the rotary screw type rather than the fulcrum lever type were determined by archaeological findings.

Additional primary source material of considerable value to reconstructing the types of furnishings at the fort included the Bent, St. Vrain & Company trade ledgers housed in the Pierre Chouteau Collection at the Missouri Historical Society in Saint Louis. The company ledgers are extant for the years 1838 through 1841 and contain brief entries for subsequent years. By and large, the ledgers listed the goods of the Indian and Santa Fe trades and were, therefore, of paramount importance to furnishing the trade room.[4]

A valuable research tool, also at the Missouri Historical Society in the Pierre Chouteau Maffitt Collection, was the list of goods purchased by Bent, St. Vrain & Company in 1838 from Fort Jackson on the South Platte River when the latter concern went out of business. The three sections of the list were headed "Unpacked Goods," "Tools that have been in use at Fort Jackson," and "Kitchen ware that has been in use." It was assumed that these items were put into continued use at Bent's Old Fort. A third inventory that added to the primary source

---

[1] Enid T. Thompson and Sarah Olson, "Furnishing Study, Bent's Old Fort National Historic Site, Colorado," typescript, March 1974, Office of Historic Preservation, Denver Service Center, National Park Service (NPS); Sarah Olson, "Furnishing Plan for Bent's Old Fort National Historic Site," typescript, 1976, Rocky Mountain Regional Office, Denver, NPS. The Harper's Ferry Center and the superintendent and the staff members of Bent's Old Fort National Historic Site assisted the author in the furnishing process.

[2] Jackson W. Moore, Jr., *Bent's Old Fort: An Archeological Study* (Denver and Boulder, Colo.: State Historical Society of Colorado and Pruett Publishing Co., 1973).

[3] Dwight E. Stinson, Jr., "Bent's Old Fort, Historic Structure Report, Historical Data Section," typescript, 1965, NPS, p. 30.

[4] Ledger Z, May 1838-July 1838, pp. 426-33; Ledger DD, 16 April 1839-July 1840, pp. 391-96; Ledger DD, July 1841, pp. 391-96, Pierre Chouteau Collection, Missouri Historical Society, Saint Louis (hereinafter cited as MHS).

material was a brief customs list of goods brought into Taos by Charles Bent in 1842, presumably from Bent's Old Fort.[5]

Known travelers' accounts dealing with Bent's Old Fort number twenty-five, and they contain a mixed body of source material, ranging from only brief references to the fort to the detailed drawings and extensive comments made by Lieutenant Abert. Thirteen of the twenty-five sources were associated with the United States Army and seven of these army-associated informants arrived at the fort in 1846 with the Army of the West. The balance of the eyewitness reports came from independent travelers or one-time fort employees.

Two relatively comprehensive accounts of the fort are those of William M. Boggs and George Bent. Unfortunately, the usefulness of these sources was limited by the fact that they postdated the fort by several decades. Boggs spent the winter of 1844-45 trading for Bent, St. Vrain & Company. He was eighteen years old at the time. The Boggs sketches and notes were not made until 1903, fifty-eight years after his stay at the fort. George Bent, the son of William Bent, is believed to have been born at the fort in 1843 and to have resided there until the fort was abandoned in 1849. In later years, Bent was interviewed extensively by the noted historians of the Cheyenne, George Bird Grinnell and George Hyde. George Bent's recollection of the fort was drawn by George Bird Grinnell in 1908. The particular merit of the Boggs and the Bent drawings was, for the furnishing purposes, their identification of the fort rooms. However, the room locations as indicated on these drawings also engendered much confusion, since they did not always conform to the archaeological data.[6]

The most accurate, detailed accounts of Bent's Old Fort are those of James William Abert and Susan Shelby Magoffin. Susan Magoffin was a Kentucky gentlewoman who accompanied her trader husband to the fort, arriving just in advance of the Army of the West. Her diary stands as the single female account of the fort and also as one of the best accounts of Santa Fe in 1846. Abert, a lieutenant in the United States Corps of Topographical Engineers, spent time at the fort during the summer of 1845 outfitting an exploratory expedition that was a subsidiary of John C. Frémont's expedition to the Canadian River. Abert returned to the fort with the Army of the West in 1846, remaining there for six weeks in order to recover from an illness contracted during his journey across the plains. In January 1847 Abert again briefly visited the fort. His journals include both written and graphic descriptions of the site.[7]

An Abert watercolor of a portion of the council room.

Several of Abert's watercolors depict members of the fort's population but, most importantly, two watercolors from this collection are the only extant interior scenes of the fort. One of the interior scenes shows a 7 August 1845 scalp dance, held in the plaza of the fort in celebration of a Cheyenne victory over the Pawnee. The second watercolor, depicting a council of the Cheyenne and the Delaware that occurred two days after the scalp dance, includes an interior view of one corner of the council room. This view, taken together with verbal accounts, made the council room the best documented room in the fort.

As it was apparently one of the few public areas in the structure, the council room rarely escaped notice from travelers. Describing the room in his journal, Lieutenant Abert commented: "We were all seated on buffalo robes upon the ground, so ranged around the council chamber that our backs could be supported against the wall." Susan Magoffin referred to this room as the "parlor":

> They have one large room as a parlor; there are no chairs but a cushion next the wall on two sides, so the company set [sic] all round in a circle. There is no other furniture than a table on which stands a bucket of water, free to all. Any water that may be left in the cup after drinking is unceremoniously tossed onto the floor.

5 "Inventory of Merchandise, Utensils, Buffaloe Robes, Furs and Live Stock formerly belonging to Messers Sarpy & Fraeb delivered Messers Bent, St. Vrain & Co. at Platte River [sic], October 24, 1838," Pierre Chouteau Maffitt Collection, MHS; "Customs List, Charles Bent, Taos, 1842," Ritch Collection, Huntington Library, Pasadena, California.

6 William M. Boggs, "Recollections of Bent's Fort and Southern Colorado," Boggs Manuscript Collection, Documentary Resources Department, SHSC; George Bird Grinnell, *Bent's Old Fort and Its Builders* (Topeka: Kansas State Historical Society, 1923).

7 Susan Shelby Magoffin, *Down the Santa Fe Trail and into Mexico: The Diary of Susan Shelby Magoffin, 1845-1847,* ed. Stella M. Drumm (New Haven, Conn.: Yale University Press, 1926); Lieutenant James W. Abert, *Western America in 1846-1847,* ed. John Galvin (San Francisco, Calif.: John Howell Books, 1966); Abert, *Through the Country of the Comanche Indians in the Fall of the Year 1845,* ed. John Galvin (San Franciso, Calif.: John Howell Books, 1970).

The "cushion next the wall on two sides" referred to either Spanish Colonial wool sacks folded against two walls or to an adobe "banco," or bench, built on two sides of the room. The latter form of seating was illustrated in another Abert watercolor entitled, *Padre Gallegos' House, Albuquerque*.[8] The banco depicted in the Albuquerque house was covered with Spanish blankets.

Susan Magoffin described her own quarters as having "two windows one looking on the plain, the other . . . on the patio."

Susan Magoffin's room is one of the few rooms in the fort where antiques are used rather than reproductions.

Her description, together with the window arrangement shown on Abert's elevation drawings of the fort, located her room in the upper northwest corner of the fort. Susan Magoffin also listed the furniture she was carrying with her that was moved into the fort for her stay, but she included no full descriptions of these items.[9]

Most of the travelers' accounts mention the few luxury items at the fort. Few visitors, for instance, failed to note the billiard

*In 1846 the billiard room would have been
the center of considerable activity.*

table, and most remarked upon the dining facilities. Francis
Parkman took special notice of the castors and the white table-
cloth in the dining room.[10] However, the unremarkable objects
that were the basic tools for frontier existence were rarely described and the reconstruction of these had to be pieced together
from the comparative research that constituted the main
sources for the "Furnishing Plan." The large body of comparative data that went into the formation of a complete "Furnishing
Plan" for Bent's Old Fort was made up, on the one hand, of
information gathered from contemporary descriptions, both
verbal and graphic, of sites and situations similar to Bent's Old
Fort and, on the other hand, of modern studies dealing with the
decorative arts on the American frontier. (While comparative
data that relates to the trade room is discussed later in this
article, an example of the basic premises that guided the overall
selection of the fort's furnishings is included here.)

[8] Abert, *Through the Country of the Comanche Indians,* p. 3; Magoffin, *Down the Santa Fe Trail,* p. 61; Abert, *Western America in 1846-1847,* facing p. 40.

[9] Magoffin, *Down the Santa Fe Trail,* pp. 6, 60; Abert, "two exterior views," pl. 4, 1845; Abert, "interior view," pl. 8, reproduced in Dwight E. Stinson, Jr., "Bent's Old Fort, Historic Structure Report."

[10] Francis Parkman, *The Oregon Trail: Sketches of Prairie and Rocky Mountain Life* (New York: Macmillan Co., 1914), p. 271.

Because the primary function of Bent, St. Vrain & Company was the transportation and the exchange of goods, current styles of furniture, similar to various trade goods, could have arrived from Saint Louis in a matter of months. While there are no extant records of expenditures on furniture by Bent, St. Vrain & Company, there is documentation that the American Fur Company purchased several pieces of furniture from Saint Louis cabinetmakers in the 1820s.[11] However, freighting space was at a premium in caravans departing Saint Louis, limiting somewhat the importation of eastern furniture. Much of the fort furniture was probably homemade, according to the Spanish Colonial styles with which the fort's labor force was most familiar, or it was simply improvised out of surplus materials not originally intended for furniture. Indeed, improvisation was

Ration boxes make very useful and convenient tables.

highly characteristic of the frontier experience. Traveling to Fort Inge, Texas, in 1844 Lydia Spencer Lane was carrying with her six Windsor chairs purchased in Corpus Christi where they had recently come into vogue. But, more significant is the fact that Mrs. Lane was also keeping house with makeshift items of

[11] In 1828 Saint Louis cabinetmaker Beriah Cleland sold a "portable desk" to the American Fur Company; Spencer and Danial, also of Saint Louis, sold twelve "common chairs" to the same company in 1831 (Charles Van Ravenswaay, "The Anglo-American Cabinetmakers of Missouri, 1800-1835," *Missouri Historical Society Bulletin* 14 [April 1958]: 253, 255).

[12] Lydia Spencer Lane, *I Married a Soldier; or, Old Days in the Old Army,* foreword Mrs. Dwight D. Eisenhower (Albuquerque, N. Mex.: Horn & Wallace, 1964), pp. 30, 175-76, 34, 68, 182; James Josiah Webb, *Adventures in the Santa Fe Trade, 1844-1847,* ed. Ralph P. Bieber (Philadelphia, Penn.: Porcupine Press, 1974), p. 93; Magoffin, *Down the Santa Fe Trail,* p. 6.

furniture. At Fort Seldon, New Mexico, in 1869 she was using a washstand invented from a hogshead in which china had been packed. In 1844 James Josiah Webb described a similar makeshift situation in Santa Fe where he dined regularly on a dry goods box with "brown domestic tucked over for a table-cloth." This practice of "making do" is pointed out further by the fact that Susan Magoffin, along with her several pieces of furniture, was using a carpet of sail duck. Lydia Spencer Lane had a similar carpet several years later at Fort Marcy made from an "old tentfly."[12] Thus, the "Furnishing Plan" attempted to strike a reasonable balance between the markedly different interiors of early nineteenth-century New Mexico and the eastern United States and, at the same time, to allow for those improvisational practices that were unique to frontier situations.

An important appendix to the "Furnishing Plan" was the set of floor plans and elevations prepared for each room in the fort.

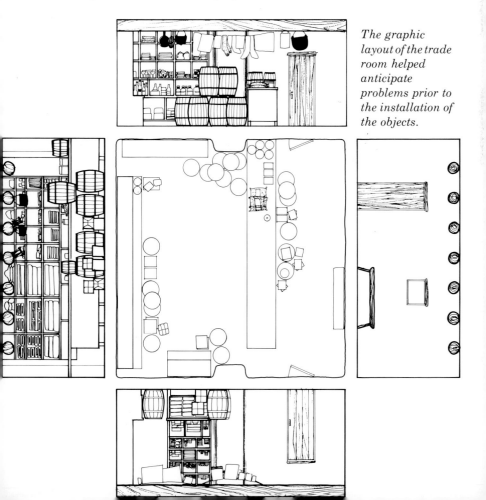

The graphic layout of the trade room helped anticipate problems prior to the installation of the objects.

The graphic explication of the subject served to clarify and to organize the lists of recommended objects. As the reconstruction of the fort had not yet begun, the drawings also established a sense of scale for the project and helped to anticipate some of the numerous problems that were to arise as objects were installed in the reconstructed fort. For instance, the graphic layout of the windows aided in determining the amount of light available in each room and, thus, guided the placement of objects. In a few cases small scale models were built of rooms and their respective furnishings, making it easier to determine the quantities of such items as produce bags, barrels, and boxes needed to interpret a given space.

Finally, the "Furnishing Plan" recommended, for a number of reasons, that reproductions be used for most of the fort's furnishings. It was felt that the furnishings should be consistent with the reproduction fabric of the building itself. And, as many of the objects arriving at the fort were newly manufactured in 1846, it was determined that reproduction material would transmit the appearance of Bent's Old Fort in the 1840s more accurately than antiques. Security was a major factor. While reproductions are often more expensive than antiques, they are replaceable. Finally, several of the objects were unavailable in antique form or, where great numbers of one item were required, only a single antique example of that item was available. The recommended trade goods alone numbered well over thirty thousand objects. More specifically, there was documentation for the importation, during a single trade year, of more than sixteen hundred butcher knives and nearly three hundred iron kettles, not to mention numerous brass and copper kettles. The acquisition of such quantities in antique form was not feasible, whereas it was possible to represent large quantities of such items as butcher knives through the combined display of reproduced knives and knife boxes.

The trade room and the fur storage room are the richest in content, and they required the greatest amount of research and reconstruction effort. The center room on the east side of the fort has been refurnished as the fort trade room while one of the rooms across the plaza from the trade room is now the fur storage room. Much of the documentation that served as the basis for the reconstruction of these two interiors is contained in the following pages and should be viewed as typifying the research stage of the furnishing process as it developed for each room in the fort.

Establishing the location for the trade room engendered considerable confusion at the outset. It involved distinguishing between the trade and the storage areas that were often mentioned interchangeably in contemporary accounts of Bent's Old Fort. Susan Magoffin observed "a little store" at the fort in 1846 as did George R. Gibson, an officer in the Missouri Volunteers, who referred to a "store, which is filled with articles for the Indian trade." And George F. Ruxton, at the fort in 1847, mentioned a "large room," one of three, seemingly contiguous, that was "used as a store and magazine."[13]

Store, storehouse, and warehouse areas were shown on both the William M. Boggs and the George Bent renderings of the fort. Boggs designated the west rooms, both upper and lower, a "large storehouse" and also referred to the middle east room as a "store room." The "trader's room," indicated by Boggs on the west end of the south row of rooms, probably referred to a trader's quarters rather than to an area for trading. George Bent labeled the lower west row of rooms as a "warehouse" and the northeast rooms as "store and warehouse." The latter rooms, constituting part of the 1845 additions to the fort, were absent on the Boggs drawings.

The artifact material in the three northeast rooms confirmed that their use was either trade or storage associated and a similar use for the center east room was established by evidence of foundations for a sales counter.[14] Due to its size and the presence of counter foundations, this last room was chosen as the one to be refurnished as the fort trade room. It seems likely that either the northwest row of rooms replaced the center east room as the central trade area after the 1845 alterations, or that all four rooms served the Indian trade simultaneously, but in different capacities. For instance, the most sought after trade items, such as whiskey and weaponry, may have been handled in an area separate from the less valuable commodities.

It was decided that the west row of rooms — the "large storehouse" or "warehouse" area indicated by Boggs and Bent — would be refurnished as warehouses on the lower level with quarters above. The Boggs and the Bent drawings were judged erroneous in their descriptions of this area of the fort as a single, undivided space, as both Lieutenant Abert's drawings and the

---

[13] Magoffin, *Down the Santa Fe Trail*, p. 60; Ralph P. Bieber, ed., *Journal of a Soldier under Kearny and Doniphan* (Glendale, Calif.: Arthur H. Clark Co., 1931), pp. 167-69; George F. Ruxton, *Life in the Far West*, ed. LeRoy R. Hafen (Norman, Okla.: University of Oklahoma Press, 1951), p. 179.

[14] Moore, *Bent's Old Fort*, pp. 21-24, 28.

archaeological survey indicated several separate, albeit large, rooms here. A second-story storage area seemed unlikely given the inconvenience that would have been caused by hauling goods in and out of storage, and considering the weight of such stored materials as furs. Furthermore, the location of Susan Magoffin's room on the upper story of the west side implied a similar use, as quarters, for the adjacent rooms. While it was impossible to document the separate functions of the storage rooms on the lower level, the northernmost of these was the best candidate for the fur storage room because of its relatively cool and ventilated location in the fort.

Only three drawings of the interiors of American fur trade stores dating from prior to the Civil War have come to light in connection with this project: Father Nicolas Point's 1847 interior of a post on the Upper Missouri River; H.B. Möllhausen's 1852 drawing of a post at Belle Vue, Nebraska; and a watercolor of a post at Yellow Lake, Wisconsin, executed between 1856 and 1860 by Franz Hölzlhuber. The Möllhausen view includes very few trade goods, focusing instead upon several Indians grouped around Möllhausen and trader Pierre Sarpy. The drawing suggests a relatively open area for trade, devoid of counters

The Möllhausen drawing is in the Museum für Völkerkunde, West Berlin.

or shelving. It is likely that the trade goods were stored elsewhere and brought into the trading area for immediate exchange. The Father Point and Hölzlhuber views, on the other hand, both feature shelves heavily laden with goods. Hölzlhuber's watercolor shows, along the back wall, a combination of open, rectangular box shelves and small, square drawers. The shelving in the Point watercolor consists of long, open shelves that appear to be free standing. While neither of these scenes show a counter, both include a work table. These two views impart an impression of overcrowdedness dominated by the primary medium of exchange for the trade goods — furs. Some furs are piled on the floor, others are hanging in clusters from the ceiling. Interestingly enough, the piled furs, occupying the entire foreground of the Point interior, are intermixed with point blankets, suggesting that, like the furs, the point blankets were incoming goods. Judging from these illustrations, the counter that ran the entire length of the Bent's Old Fort trade room may have been an unusually sophisticated feature for an early nineteenth-century trade room.

The "Furnishing Plan" recommended supplementing the trade room counter space with shelves along three walls of the room. The additional shelving was required to accommodate the large volume of trade goods that formed the yearly trading outfit for Bent, St. Vrain & Company and to re-create the overcrowdedness evident in the period drawings. It was decided that the shelves should approximate those in a Hudson's Bay Company post described as "box shelves, nearly two feet deep."[15] The goods displayed within the trade room are both the most important and the best documented group of objects exhibited in the refurnished fort. Beyond their object significance they represent both the three-cornered trade for which Bent, St. Vrain & Company operated and the various populations that participated in that trade.

The most helpful source for stocking the shelves were the lists of goods purchased by Bent, St. Vrain & Company from Pierre Chouteau, Jr., in Saint Louis. Additional primary information about the trade goods was contained in the list of goods transferred from Fort Jackson to Bent, St. Vrain & Company in 1838 and in a customs list of goods brought into Taos by Charles

---

[15] H. M. Robinson, *The Great Fur Land; or, Sketches of Life in the Hudson's Bay Territory*, 5th ed. (New York: G.P. Putnam's Sons, 1879), cited in *Lower Fort Garry National Historical Park* (Ottawa, Canada: Dept. of Northern Affairs and National Resources, National Park Branch, 1967), p. 6.

Bent in 1842. Also of some use were comments from travelers describing the exchange of goods at the fort, although all of these were only cursory accounts of that trade.

It was assumed that some of the items on the list of goods purchased by Bent, St. Vrain & Company in 1840 were retained for use at the fort although there was no indication which items merely passed through the fort and which were actually put into use there. Certainly the major part of the outfit was designated for trade, although items listed singly may have been intended for special uses as was the halter labeled "for Wm. Bent."

The primary tasks of the furnishings specialist lay in identifying precisely each object listed and in determining the appropriate forms of exterior packaging for many of those objects. Most of the goods were described in no more detail than their generic object designation. Manufacturers' names were included in a few cases and some further information was provided by the distinctions made as to place of origin. At the end of the 1838 list a clear distinction was made among advances on English, New York, and Saint Louis goods. However, within the body of the lists those goods designated "N.Y." were of both American and English manufacture. The remainder of the goods were probably available from retailers in Saint Louis. The prices of objects also helped in identifying them, particularly in instances where several grades of one object were ordered. Various museum collections, such as that of the Museum of the Fur Trade at Chadron, Nebraska, were an important resource for identifying trade goods as were the records of larger trading companies operating during the same period as Bent, St. Vrain & Company, such as the American Fur Company records at Saint Louis and Hudson's Bay Company records at Winnipeg, Canada.

Large portions of the lists of trade goods consisted of decorative trinkets, such as feathers, gartering, arm and hat bands, rings, ribbons, gorgets, looking glasses, bells, wampum moons, and several descriptions of beads. Most of these items were exclusive to the Indian trade and were put to a wide variety of decorative uses by the Indians. Some of the decorative accessories listed on the trade ledgers can be identified in contemporary drawings of Indians that traded in the area of the fort. A strikingly Anglo form of gartering shows up in George Catlin's drawing of a Kiowa Indian. While only solid colored gartering was invoiced in the 1840 trade ledgers, the Kiowa is probably wearing what was designated on the 1839 list as "Highland

These Catlin drawings of Kiowa show some of the decorative accessories that were traded—the "Highland Gartering," wrist bands, and arm bands.

Gartering." The Kiowa is also wearing a wrist band, and wrist bands appear only on the 1838 list. Like the arm bands listed in 1840, wrist bands were ordered in pairs. A complete pair of arm bands appears in another Catlin drawing of a Kiowa.

It was difficult to identify exact materials for all of the metallic ornaments traded by Bent, St. Vrain & Company. The 1838 and 1839 trade ledgers contained entries for several dozen arm and wrist bands of unspecified materials, while the 1840 list specified a few arm bands of silver. Although a single silver gorget was entered on the 1840 list, the two dozen gorgets ordered in 1839 were tin, and similarly the majority of arm and wrist bands traded were probably tin. Some museum collections also contain early nineteenth-century Plains Indian ornaments of brass and German silver. German silver became widely used only after 1860, but its early use at Bent's Old Fort was documented by an entry on the 1841 list for three pounds of German silver.[16]

The gorget worn by the Kiowa Indian in Catlin's drawing is shell rather than metallic. It was probably Indian made from conch or abalone shell. There is ample documentation for conch and abalone shells having been traded to the Plains Indians in

---

[16] James Austin Hanson, *Metal Weapons, Tools, and Ornaments of the Teton Dakota Indians* (Lincoln: University of Nebraska Press, 1975), p. 75.

the first half of the nineteenth century.[17] In 1841 Bent, St. Vrain & Company ordered twelve pounds of seashells. Wampum moons were shipped in great numbers to the fort each year, and wampum shells appeared on the 1839 list. Trade shells were put to a variety of uses as is evident from a drawing of a Sioux Indian done by Lieutenant Abert in August 1845. The sketch was done along the banks of the Arkansas River just outside the walls of Bent's Fort. The Sioux Indian was wearing what appears to be a conch shell moon, or disc, as a hair ornament.

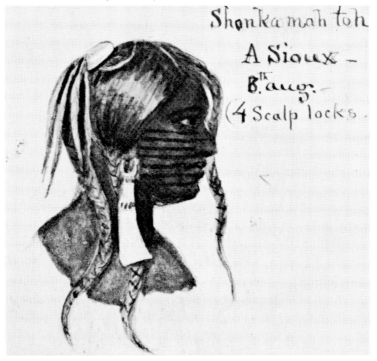

Shonka mah toh
A Sioux —
B.tk auy. —
(4 Scalp locks.

The shells invoiced on the Bent, St. Vrain & Company trade ledgers were usually listed in sets. Sets of any given object seemed to have indicated a graduation in size. "30 Setts Hair Plates" appeared on the 1841 list, and these ornaments can be seen hanging down the right shoulder of the Kiowa Indian. The use of hairplates was unique to the Plains Indians and occurred only prior to 1868.[18]

---

[17] Charles Hanson, Jr., "The Abalone Shell as a Trade Item," *Museum of the Fur Trade Quarterly* 9 (Fall 1973): 8-10.

[18] J. A. Hanson, *Metal Weapons, Tools, and Ornaments of the Teton Dakota Indians*, p. 93.

In addition to the several manufactured or ready-made ornaments that were traded to the Indians, a limitless potential for handmade accessories was offered by the several varieties of hardware and raw material that appeared on the trade ledgers. The earrings depicted in both of the Catlin drawings and in another Abert drawing of a Sioux Indian do not fit descriptions for factory-made earrings and were probably fashioned out of tinware or copper items and brass wire. The Brulé Sioux in the Abert drawing is wearing what is clearly a machine-made linen

shirt, and Abert described the ornamentation on his buffalo robe cape as a combination of quillwork and tufts of red worsted.[19] The shirt could well have come from one of the Bent, St. Vrain & Company trade outfits, and the red worsted could have come from the four and three-quarter pounds of scarlet yarn entered on the 1839 list.

A significant portion of the trade ledgers consist of point blankets, and it is evident from the 1840 list that the three-

[19] Abert, *Through the Country of the Comanche Indians,* entry for 8 August 1845.

point, white blanket was the most in demand. The distinction was made on the 1840 list between Hudson's Bay and other blankets, denoting that the former came from the same English manufacturers used by the Hudson's Bay Company. There were doubtless other objects traded by Bent, St. Vrain & Company that were identical to Hudson's Bay goods. Chief Factor John McLoughlin wrote from Fort Vancouver in 1843 that both English and American traders "supply Indians with the same kind of articles, and some of them procured from the same Manufacturers."[20]

During the 1840s the Hudson's Bay Company secured their point blankets from at least three different woolen mills with most of the contracts being awarded to either J. Early & Sons of Witney or to A. & S. Henry & Company of Leeds. There is evidence that in 1843 Henry & Company supplied the American Fur Company in addition to the Hudson's Bay Company.[21]

The non-Hudson's Bay blankets listed on the Bent, St. Vrain & Company ledgers were probably of American manufacture. There is ample documentation for the American manufacture of point blankets in the Hudson's Bay Company archives, the American version having been described as distinct in both color and texture. Addressing the London office in 1842, John McLoughlin reported that "the American Blanket though generally inferior to ours, meets a readier sale with Indians in consequence of its gaudy color, and we beg that those we have ordered may be made in respect of color and texture fully equal to the sample [of the American blankets] sent."[22] Subsequent communications between the London office and the posts indicated that the English manufacturers were unable to match the brilliancy of the American reds, and an 1844 entry in the London correspondence to English tradespeople noted that the brilliancy of the American red was due to the manner in which it was dressed. Several years later, mention was made of the difference in the American and English blue point blanket. A Hudson's Bay post complained to the London office that the color of the English blankets sent in 1855 was too deep a blue, and

---

[20] "The Letters of John McLoughlin from Fort Vancouver to the Governor and Committee, Second Series, 1839-44," *Hudson's Bay Record Society,* vol. 6, 4 December 1843, p. 187.

[21] An 18 June 1843 letter from the London office of the Hudson's Bay Company to A & S Henry & Company acknowledged the receipt of a comparative statement of prices and quality for blankets supplied to both the Hudson's Bay Company and the American Fur Company (Hudson's Bay Company Archives, A. 5/14, folio 164).

[22] "The Letters of John McLoughlin from Fort Vancouver to the Governor and Committee, Second Series, 1839-44," 31 October 1842, 6:92.

that they were unpopular with the Indians who preferred the *"very light sky blue* color" obtained from the American traders.[23]

Letters from the London office to English manufacturers also contained such information as standard dimensions and weights for the point blankets; standard widths for the head stripe along with a prescribed margin from the end of the blanket to the head stripe; and directions for baling the blankets.[24] An average of twenty-five blankets constituted a bale, and a single blanket was used as a wrapper for the baled blankets in addition to an outside covering. The point blankets ordered by Bent, St. Vrain & Company were probably baled in a similar manner as there was an entry on the 1838 list for two, two and one-half point white wrappers. During the nineteenth century, both English and American point blankets were manufactured in double lengths, thus the "pr.," or pairs, blankets on the trade lists.

Finally, the Hudson's Bay Company archives contained directions for marking baled blankets. Information required on the outside of the bales included the date of the outfit, initials designating both the Hudson's Bay Company and the central post to which the blankets were being sent, and the number of the bale. This marking system was, in fact, identical to that used by the outposts on bales of furs. American Fur Company orders always included the markings for such packages; it can only be assumed that a similar system was used by Bent and St. Vrain.[25]

The point blankets at Bent's Old Fort would have been counterbalanced by the presence of Spanish Colonial Rio Grande blankets and Navajo blankets. Thomas J. Farnham who traveled to Bent's Old Fort in 1839 observed that the proprietors of the fort slept on pallets of straw and Spanish blankets.[26] The Spanish, or Rio Grande, blankets mentioned by Farnham were items of exchange traded far beyond the confines of the Bent's

[23] Hudson's Bay Company Archives, A. 5/14, folio 307, 29 July 1844; A. 64/58, folio 201, September 1857.

[24] Ibid., A. 5/13, folio 268, 10 November 1844; A. 5/14, folio 185, 13 September 1843; A. 64/58, folio 65d, 1855.

[25] Ibid., A. 5/14, folio 2, 27 April 1842; John A. Hussey, "Historic Structure Report, Historical Data Section, Fort Vancouver National Historic Site, Washington," vol. 2, typescript, NPS, 1976, p. 13; Charles E. Hanson, Jr., Museum of the Fur Trade, Chadron, Nebraska, to Cathryne Johnson, State Historical Society of Colorado, Denver, 26 August 1977.

[26] Thomas J. Farnham, *Travels in the Great Western Prairies* (New York: Greeley & McElrath, 1843), p. 37.

The furnishings in Abert's quarters provide warmth and comfort and include a buffalo skin rug and a Rio Grande bed covering.

Old Fort area. Josiah Gregg had remarked upon this trade earlier in the 1830s:

> The new Mexicans are celebrated for the manufacture of coarse blankets, which is an article of considerable traffic between them and the southern provinces, as also with the neighboring Indians, and on some occasions with the United States. The finer articles are curiously woven in handsome figures of various colors. These are of different qualities, the most ordinary being valued at about two dollars apiece, while those of the finest texture, especially their imitations of the "Sarape Navajo," will sell for twenty dollars or more.[27]

The presence of the Navajo blanket at Bent's Old Fort is documented by the Lieutenant Abert watercolor of the Cheyenne scalp dance. Abert described the dancers as consisting of "about forty women with faces painted red and black, nearly all cloaked with Navajo blankets." In the 1840s most Navajo blankets were woven in stripes as shown in this drawing.[28]

The cotton yard goods entered on the 1840 list probably came from the United States with the exception of the furniture prints, or chintz, and the "English" calico. An 1840 edition of Hunt's *Merchant's Magazine and Commercial Review* listed thirty-six "Calico Printing" factories in this country, all located in New England.[29] Some of these factories were probably printing cloth that was itself imported. The light ground Merrimack prints that appeared on the 1839 ledger and the Merrimack calico invoiced in 1841 were traced to the Merrimack Manufacturing Company in Lowell, Massachusetts. A trade card for this

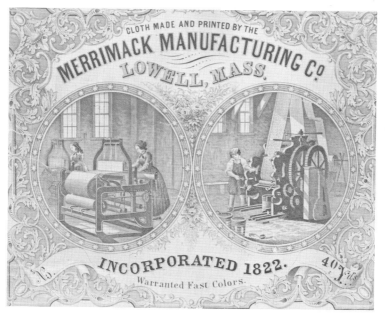

company is extant in the American Antiquarian Society, and not only is the card a prototype for yard good labels, but it also clearly illustrates the printed pattern on a length of cloth coming off a printing machine.

Other manufacturers that were identified on the trade ledgers included the John Wilson Manufactory of Sheffield, England, and the Collins & Company of Collinsville, Connecticut. The axes manufactured by Collins & Company were intended

[27] Josiah Gregg, *Commerce of the Prairies* (Dallas, Tex.: Southwest Press, 1933) pp. 136-137.

[28] Abert, *Through the Country of the Comanche Indians,* p. 4; C. E. Hanson, Jr., to C. Johnson, 26 August 1977.

[29] [Freeman Hunt], *Merchant's Magazine and Commercial Review* [New York], 1840.

primarily as tools rather than as trade axes, and the relatively small quantities of Collins "best" axes that appeared on the trade lists were therefore probably designated for Anglo use rather than as trade objects.[30]

Seven entries for gunpowder appeared on the Bent, St. Vrain & Company lists between 1838 and 1841. While powder was part of each yearly outfit, this is one item that would have been stored separately in a powder magazine rather than in the trade room. All of the powder was ordered in 50-pound kegs. Four of the seven orders were for duPont powder, and two distinct grades of duPont powder appear on the 1840 list. The three entires that did not specify a maker were probably also duPont powder as the prices correlated with the duPont entries.

The establishment of the duPont Company as a supplier to Bent, St. Vrain & Company was one of the most useful references found on the trade ledgers. The records of the duPont Company housed at the Hagley Museum in Greenville, Delaware, provided all of the necessary information for the reproduction of powder kegs — from letters to coopers containing specifications for kegs to artwork for the keg labels.[31] The duPont label matched an 1839 entry on the Bent, St. Vrain & Company ledgers for "Eagle Powder."

Like the duPont powder, most of the items on the trade lists would have exhibited some sort of manufacturer's label. As the majority of objects had no factory designations, manufacturers were established primarily through period advertisements contained in collections of trade cards and advertising posters. As contrasted to the multi-color processes that followed the Civil War, early nineteenth-century labels were printed in only one color, most typically in black and white, making the reproduction process relatively simple. However, it was not feasible economically to repeat the lithographic process by which such labels were originally printed.

One of the most elusive problems was determining how the trade goods were packaged when they arrived at Bent's Old Fort. Just as brown wrapping paper is not a highly collectable item today, historic packing materials rarely have been saved, let alone collected. Fortunately, early nineteenth-century advertisements often illustrated products packaged as they emerged from the factory. Similar pictorial documents were also found on occasional factory invoices. Even so, the fact that the available data was not sufficient to package accurately all of the items exhibited is exemplary of the many compromises that were part of refurnishing the trade room.

A primary consideration in packing trade goods for shipment west was space. The "nests" of kettles and trunks on the trade lists attest to this concern. One Hudson's Bay Company post based its choice of tinware on the way it was packed — a manufacturer that packed ten tin kettles and their lids in a single nest being preferred to one that packed the kettles and lids in separate nests.[32] It was also evident from the fort's ledgers that small goods were either sewn onto cards or packed in papers, such as the "Papers Hawk Bells" that appeared on the 1840 list.

Exterior packaging mentioned on the Bent, St. Vrain & Company lists over a four-year period included boxes, bags, barrels, and bales, although the type of packaging specified for each item was rarely consistent from one year to the next. Yard goods and clothing were usually baled, but in at least two instances they were shipped in three-gallon and five-gallon, iron

---

[30] Harold L. Peterson, *American Indian Tomahawks* (New York: Museum of the American Indian, Heye Foundation 1971), p. 46.

[31] duPont Company, Letter Books, Eleutherian Mills Historical Library, Greenville, Delaware.

[32] Hudson's Bay Company Archives. A. 64/58, folio 32d, 1860-61.

bound kegs. As for bale wrappers, one of the materials ordered by the Hudson's Bay Company for baling purposes was "strong, stout Osnaburg," a type of coarse linen, originally made in Osnaburg, Germany. The Osnaburg linen ordered by Bent, St. Vrain & Company was probably also used for this purpose, but the American Fur Company bales were usually covered with ordinary canvas. For expensive cloths like stroud, oil cloth was wrapped around the outside. Evidence also exists of bale wrappers being secured in the field. Many of the goods transferred from Fort Jackson in 1838 arrived in bales bound up by buffalo robes, and records of the Santa Fe trade in the 1820s indicated the use of the domestic woolen fabric "jerga" as baling material.[33]

The distribution of the several varieties of trade goods was inspired by a single preoccupation, the trade in furs. The fur trade was built on beaver pelts, the undercoat fur of which made a fine napped felt particularly adapted to the production of beaver hats. By the late seventeenth-century "beavers" were a mark of high fashion, the several styles of Van Dycks, Tricorns, and Wellingtons evolving into probably the most famous beaver of them all, the "topper." No doubt, the twelve "Black Fur" hats that were part of Bent, St. Vrain & Company's 1840 inventory were top hats. They were purchased at £ 1.74, or $8.75 and, by 1841, this desirable article had risen to £ 2.75, or $13.75. By 1850 the demand for beaver hats had all but exhausted its source of supply in the New World. Substitutes for beaver, particularly marten and muskrat, were experimented with, none too successfully, by European haberdashers, and the beaver top hat finally gave way to the silk top hat.[34]

Only passing references remain to the volumes of furs traded at Bent's Old Fort, with the exception of a full return for the winter season of 1842.[35] This return showed the company at the transition point between the beaver trade and the trade in buffalo, upon which the American fur trade subsisted for another three decades.

The 1842 season produced 1,670 beaver skins of three gradations in quality, the total valued at $7,836.12. Among these

[33] Hudson's Bay Company Archives, A. 5/13, folio 178, 18 March 1841; George Champlin Sibley, *Account Books*, cited in E. Boyd, *Popular Arts of Spanish New Mexico* (Santa Fe: Museum of New Mexico Press, 1974), p. 185; C. E. Hanson, Jr. to C. Johnson, 26 August 1977.

[34] E. E. Rich, *The History of the Hudson's Bay Company, 1670-1870*, vol. 1 (London: Hudson's Bay Record Society, 1958), pp. 388-89.

[35] Journal EE, 22 July 1842, p. 246, Chouteau-Maffitt Collection, MHS.

The well-stocked trade room documents the primary purpose of the fort.

were seventeen "old coats," the coat beaver being a dried skin that had been worn for some time, usually by the Indians. The coat beaver had its own value, because by the time it reached the European market it had lost its long outer fur, leaving the undercoat of wool immediately accessible for processing.[36]

While the buffalo returns for the season far outnumbered those for beaver, they brought a lower total market value. There were 2,264 "seasoned," or prime winter, robes and 395 summer robes — each again consisting of three grades — and 41 "refuse," or half robes, and 277 calf robes. The total value was $7,535.80.[37] Other skins listed on the 1842 return included 100 muskrat, 7 grizzly bear, 4 otter, and 1 mink, and additional evidence disclosed deer, wolf, bobcat, and badger also being collected in the area of the fort.

[36] Rich, *History of the Hudson's Bay Company,* pp. 47-48.

[37] Virtually all of the furs transported to New Orleans for shipment to the European markets came from the Saint Louis warehouses, and a telling note on the significance of Bent's Old Fort within the American fur trade at large are the figures compiled by Isaac Lippincott from nineteenth-century business magazines for "Buffalo Robes and Furs Received at New Orleans from the Interior." The value of 3,122 fur packs received at New Orleans in 1842 was listed as $146,000; the return from Bent, St. Vrain & Company was valued at $15,936, constituting more than ten percent of that total (Isaac Lippincott, "A Century and a Half of Fur Trade at St. Louis," *Washington University Studies: Humanistic Series,* vol. 3, pt. 2, no. 2 [April 1916]: 205-42).

The fur returns from Bent's Old Fort represented the working capital upon which Bent, St. Vrain & Company operated, and the exhibits in the fur storage room were therefore considered essential to the interpretation of the fort, despite the manifold obstacles to mounting such an exhibit in the 1970s. Given the present commitments of the United States to conservation, it was out of the question from the outset to install anything approaching the varieties of species and quantities of furs that nurtured the fur trade and, at the same time, eventually obliterated it. The current list of endangered species automatically eliminated the representation of grizzly bear and timber wolf. Further obstacles lay in the maintenance of this largely organic exhibit. It was necessary to tan fully most of the furs for permanent display, thereby sacrificing the odors and dense insect population that were doubtless the salient characteristic of the untanned furs in the 1840s fur room.

Because the methods by which the furs were brought to market were an integral part of the fur room's history, much of the research required to reconstruct this interior concentrated on early nineteenth-century practices of fur storage and packing. The Hudson's Bay Company records provided useful information on some of these processes, although it must be recognized that the practices of the American Fur Company would be a more likely model at Bent's Old Fort. John Hussey's report for the National Park Service on the 1840s fur store at Fort Vancouver gave pertinent information on fur packing, and Charles Hanson, Jr., of the Museum of the Fur Trade and an authority on American frontier practices, supplied additional data on fur packing methods more likely practiced at Bent's Old Fort.[38]

The preliminary treatment of furs was, for the most part, a field operation and most of the furs arrived at the fort already scraped and dried, undergoing full processing only upon reaching the eastern United States or the European markets. Observations made in the 1860s at one Hudson's Bay post noted that fragile furs were hung from the walls or ceiling, leaving the tougher furs lying on the floor in "huge heaps." The latter category of furs may have consisted chiefly of beaver, but in the case of Bent's Old Fort, it would have included a preponderance of buffalo robes. The stored furs required constant vigilance

---

[38] Hussey, "Historic Structure Report, Frt Vancouver," 2:8-24; C. E. Hanson, Jr. to C. Johnson, 26 August 1977.

against dampness or insects, the detected presence of which prompted immediate outdoor airing and beating.[39]

The first step in preparing for a shipment of furs eastward was to estimate the number of packs that would be required, and their total weight, so that manpower and transportation facilities could be lined up. The furs were moved by pack animals, either horses or mules, or wheeled vehicles, whether small carts or larger wagons.

Received from the field, the skins were folded in piles and weighted down in storage before being pressed into packs. Whether the press was the crude lever type used in more primitive establishments, the massive wedge type favored by the Hudson's Bay Company, or the sophisticated screw or rotary type used at Bent's Old Fort, the idea was to compress a pile of

The fur press was a necessary tool for packaging furs before shipment.

dried skins into a compact bundle or bale that could be readily hoisted and handled by employees without the aid of machines.[40]

[39] Hussey, "Historic Structure Report, Fort Vancouver," 2:17, 9.

[40] An illuminating study of the various types of presses and their mode of operation is found in Charles E. Hanson, Jr., "Robe and Fur Presses," *Museum of the Fur Trade Quarterly* 3 (Summer 1967): 3-6.

The size of the packs varied from fifty to one hundred pounds, according to circumstances. William Ashley in 1825 reported bringing in packs of around fifty pounds, consisting of around thirty beaver each, which would have been lashed onto his pack mules. With the advent of carts to the mountain rendezvous beginning in 1830, larger packs came into vogue. John McLoughlin reported that at the 1836 rendezvous at Green River, rival American Fur Company trappers brought in over fifty packs weighing around ninety pounds each. This was also the average weight of Hudson Bay Company packs sent out on shipboard. According to the records at Fort Clark on the Upper Missouri, packs of sixty beaver each averaged eighty-four pounds.[41] There is little reason to doubt that, with wagon transportation available, the Bent, St. Vrain beaver packs were mainly in this weight range. A pack of this weight might appear in the shape of a bundle roughly rectangular, about 20 by 24 inches and 12 to 16 inches thick.[42]

Buffalo robes ran ten to a pack, and probably weighed also in the range of eighty to one hundred pounds per pack. Presumably they were folded three or four times, though data on the shape and dimensions of a typical buffalo robe pack are scanty. There is eyewitness evidence that Fort Laramie fur traders sometimes transported their buffalo robes to Saint Louis in carts simply piled, spread out, one on top of the other, without packaging, but this was probably an exception to the rule, since the uncured hides would deteriorate with exposure to weather.[43] Muskrat, lynx, bear, and deer hides were among other miscellaneous items in a typical cargo, but at Bent's Old Fort beaver and buffalo predominated. The last Rocky Mountain rendezvous was held in 1840 because the beaver had been so depleted; it seems safe to assume, then, that by 1845-46 the bulk of the fort's furs by weight, if not by value, consisted of buffalo robes.

All furs were routinely folded fur-side-in to keep vermin infestation to a minimum. Some form of protective wrapping was usually placed at the top and the bottom of the pile of furs in

[41] "The Letters of John McLoughlin from Fort Vancouver to the Governor and Committee, First Series, 1825-38," *Hudson's Bay Record Society*, vol. 4, p. 209; Dale L. Morgan, ed., *The West of William H. Ashley. . . Recorded in the Diaries and Letters of William H. Ashley and His Contemporaries* (Denver, Colo.: Old West Publishing Co., 1964), p. 128; Annie Heloise Abel, ed., *Chardon's Journal at Fort Clark, 1834-1839* (Pierre: University of South Dakota Department of History and State of South Dakota, 1932), p. 324.

[42] Charles J. Hanson, Jr. interview with Merrill Mattes, Nebraska State Historical Society, Lincoln, Nebraska, cited in Mattes to C. Johnson, 6 September 1977.

[43] Abel ed., *Chardon's Journal*, p. 324; Merrill J. Mattes, *The Great Platte River Road: The Covered Wagon Mainline via Fort Kearny to Fort Laramie* (n.p.: Nebraska State Historical Society, 1969), pp. 155-56.

the press. The less valuable skins such as bear and deer, or any damaged hides, were known to be in such use at Hudson's Bay posts.[44] Buffalo robes may have been the most commonly used wrapper at Bent's Old Fort.

Pack cords were probably made from the quantities of rope, particularly manila and hemp, which were listed on the Bent, St. Vrain ledgers. In the absence of rope these may have been supplemented by cords homemade from stripped buffalo hides. Hudson's Bay practice was to lay cords under the pack before pressing, then to secure them over the top of the pack by cinching and knotting. After the pack was removed from the press, more cords were secured. The more tightly bound the pack, the less chance existed of insect penetration.[45] Whatever system of cording was used at the fort, it was intended to make a tight, tough package to withstand the rigors of journey to market.

The final stage of the process was marking the packs.[46] At Bent's Old Fort the packs were probably marked with black paint or lamp black applied with brushes. It was noted that the 1838 outfit for Bent's Old Fort included a quantity of "marking brushes." Markings were intended to identify the serial number of the pack, the date of shipment, the name or the acronym for the company, and the weight at time of shipment.[47]

Storing, preserving, pressing, packing, marking, and loading beaver skins or buffalo robes required a sizeable, able-bodied work force, if the returns were as large as they were for Bent, St. Vrain & Company in 1842. The toil and sweat that went into the colorful process can only be imagined.

While Hudson's Bay furs moved to England by ship, and the Upper Missouri furs went by mackinaw to Saint Louis, Bent's Fort furs moved mainly by cart caravan or wagon train, well-guarded. When fur traders made similar trips down the Platte River from Fort Laramie, it was observed by Oregon Trail emigrants that their battered wagons creaked and groaned with their humped loads, and the smell of hides and unwashed wagoneers was enough for all to give them a wide berth.[48] Thus,

---

[44] Hussey, "Historic Structure Report, Fort Vancouver," 2:20-21.

[45] "The Letters of John McLoughlin from Fort Vancouver to the Governor and Committee, First Series, 1825-38," 4:60.

[46] While there was evidence of the use of lead seals as a final device to discourage tampering with the packs at other fur trading posts, the archaeological survey at Bent's Old Fort uncovered no such evidence (Alan R. Woolworth, "Archaeological Excavations at the Northwest Company's Depot, Grand Portage Minnesota, in 1970-1971 by the Minnesota Historical Society," typescript, Minnesota Historical Society, Saint Paul, Minnesota, p. 123).

[47] C. E. Hanson, Jr., "Robe and Fur Presses," p. 6.

[48] Mattes, *The Great Platte River Road*, pp. 155-56.

it may have been also on the Santa Fe Trail eastbound, with the only good smell that of profits from this primitive commerce. Although some effort was made by the partners to ship their furs by homemade flatboats down the Arkansas River, that effort predictably failed because of the nature of that stream, which had more sand bars than water.[49] Thus, the special precaution with packaging for water transportation, which was a major concern with the Hudson's Bay Company sea voyages or the American Fur Company furs shipped downstream to Saint Louis, was not one of the Bent, St. Vrain problems.

As with the fur packaging situation, each area and room in the fort presented its own set of unique difficulties that had to be thought out before an adequate refurnishing plan could be formulated. This overview of a few of the research processes employed to re-create the trade room and the fur storage room at the fort covers only a limited number of examples involved in the overall refurnishing project. Many other rooms of varying nature required additional study before they could be re-created. Literally thousands of objects passed through the fort during its original existence. These commonplace items all played some part in the fort's total environment, and they had to be taken into consideration in the re-creation of that environment. Such objects are significant, because together they offer a revealing glimpse at the diversity of the fur trade and the variety of life styles involved in that trade at Bent's Old Fort.[50]

SARAH M. OLSON holds B.A. and M.A. degrees in the history of art from Scripps College and the University of Michigan, respectively. As a historian under contract with the National Park Service, she authored the furnishing plan for Bent's Old Fort and supervised the implementation of the plan.

---

[49] David Lavender, *Bent's Fort* (Garden City, N.Y.: Doubleday & Co., 1954), pp. 221, 223.

[50] An interpretive film, *Castle on the Plain*, produced by Thomas Klieman for the National Park Service with the assistance of the Harpers Ferry Center, West Virginia, is a thirty-minute, audio-visual presentation shown on television monitors at the Bent's Old Fort National Historic Site. The film, in conjunction with the re-created, refurnished fort, costumed personnel (living history), and historical literature, establishes the basis for the interpretive program at the fort.

Bibliographical Notes

A major historic reconstruction completed by the National Park Service in 1976, Bent's Old Fort is an important landmark in American westward expansion and a significant monument to an early nineteenth-century trading center. In large measure these articles focus on previously unpublished topics that pertain to the decline and to the ultimate rebuilding of this frontier outpost of American civilization. Thus, these studies contribute to a fuller realization of the history of the fort, especially in terms of the unstinting efforts at preservation that led to its detailed and authentic reconstruction.

Historical research often begins with inquiry into documents, manuscripts, and contemporary observations. While several important collections have contributed to the primary source material available on Bent's Old Fort, only the most notable collections are singled out here. Primary source materials in the Documentary Resources Department of the State Historical Society of Colorado include a Bent's Fort Collection as well as other sources related to the Bent brothers and their outpost. The Western History Collections at the University of Colorado Libraries house a Bent and St. Vrain Collection, and the Western History Department of the Denver Public Library holds the Charles W. Hurd letters about Charles Bent.

Important out-of-state collections include the very helpful Bent and St. Vrain Papers and the Pierre Chouteau Collection at the Missouri Historical Society in Saint Louis. Many useful journals and manuscripts that shed light on the fort are held by the Bancroft Library at the University of California at Berkeley and at the Huntington Library in Pasadena, California. In addition, other archival materials have contributed a foundation for historical research necessary to an extended treatment of life at Bent's Old Fort.

Through their writings, many researchers and historians have kept the fort alive over the years. Their publications provide a solid basis for all levels of study related to the fort — from general interest reading to more serious scholarly inquiry. Background literature on the fort is extensive; the site is discussed in numerous works, but only those works dealing directly with the fort are included here.

In *Bent's Old Fort and Its Builders* (Topeka: Kansas State Historical Society, 1923), George Bird Grinnell established a date for the building of the fort. He relied on information received from George Bent, the son of the fort's builder William Bent and a Southern Cheyenne, named Porcupine Bull. This aspect of Grinnell's evidence, however, was not corroborated by documents, and it contributed to a long debate over the correct year for the construction of the fort.

Other early, short studies that are helpful include edited reprints of several contemporary accounts, as well as articles, dealing with the fort and published in *The Colorado Magazine*. A few of these are: Arthur J. Fynn, "Furs and Forts of the Rocky Mountain West," 9 (January 1932); "Letters and Notes from or about Bent's Fort, 1844-1845, Copied from the *St. Louis Reveille*," 11 (November 1934); particularly enlightening is LeRoy R. Hafen, "When Was Bent's Fort Built?" 31 (April 1954); Herbert W. Dick, "The Excavation of Bent's Old Fort, Otero County, Colorado," 33 (July 1956); Arthur Woodward, "Sidelights on Bent's Old Fort," 33 (October 1956); "More about Bent's Old Fort," 34 (April 1957); and Edgeley W. Todd, "Bent's Fort in 1846," 34 (July 1957).

In 1954 David Lavender published *Bent's Fort* (Garden City, N.Y.: Doubleday & Co.). To date, Lavender's account is the most dramatic and readable treatment of the Bent brothers and their adobe castle on the banks of the Arkansas River. This was followed two years later by Nolie Mumey's limited edition of *Old Forts and Trading Posts of the West: Bent's Old Fort and Bent's New Fort on the Arkansas River,* vol. 1 (Denver, Colo.: Artcraft Press, 1956). A scholarly examination, this work contains an interesting commentary on the several contradictory stories related to the destruction of the fort. Portentously, Mumey commented that the "visible structure ⌊of the fort⌋ has faded from view, and while now recorded only on the pages of history, some day it may rise again to recall its former days of glory."

Herbert W. Dick's "The Excavation of Bent's Fort" (Trinidad, 1956), a typescript in the Documentary Resources Department of the State Historical Society of Colorado, outlines the Society's early efforts at the site after it received the scanty remains of the fort as a gift from the Daughters of the American Revolution in 1953. A local resident of the Las Animas area, Charles W. Hurd published a personalized narrative entitled *Bent's Stockade: Hidden in the Hills* (Las Animas, Colo.: By the Author, 1960) that has information on each of the Bent ventures in outpost construction. The captivating story behind the fort led to the production of an excellent and well-illustrated children's book, *Bent's Fort: Crossroads of the Great West* (Champaign, Ill.: Garrard Publishing Co., 1967) by Wyatt Blassingame.

More recently, in 1973 the specialized work *Bent's Old Fort: An Archeological Study* by Jackson W. Moore, Jr., with a historical introduction by Dwight E. Stinson, Jr., was published jointly by the Society and Pruett Publishing Company of Boulder for the National Park Service (NPS). A helpful booklet on the technicalities of planning the reconstruction is *Bent's Old Fort,* also published in 1973 by the NPS and URS/Ken R. White Company. Several other NPS studies, in manuscript form, are available for research through the NPS. And finally, two recent articles in the Colorado Centennial issue of *American West,* vol. 13 (September/October 1976) were devoted to the history and the reconstruction of Bent's Old Fort. Walter Briggs and Glenn Cuerden in "Castle in the Desert" present a historical tour of the reconstructed fort, and Ferol Egan in "Frémont at Bent's Fort" discusses that explorer's 1844 visit to the adobe outpost.

A review of the above literature in conjunction with these articles reveals three distinct periods in the history of Bent's Old Fort: the original structure and its functions; the century of the partial use, abandonment, and decline, with early endeavors to preserve and to mark the remains of a pioneer enterprise; and the numerous facets of the reconstruction project itself. To comprehend fully the significance of the fort, the two latter phases of its existence cannot be overlooked. Fulfilling Nolie Mumey's prediction of twenty years ago, Bent's Old Fort has risen again "to recall its former days of glory."

Picture Credits

Cover, title page, photos by Glenn Cuerden, Cuerden Advertising Design, Denver, Colorado; 1, artwork by Karen Williamson, Denver (State Historical Society of Colorado [SHSC]); 2, 3, 4, 5, 1976 photos by the National Park Service (NPS); 6 and 7, artwork by Karen Williamson (SHSC); 8 and 9, map of the Santa Fe Trail, compiled by W.E. Brown, United States Department of the Interior, National Park Service (NPS); 10, 12, 14, 17, SHSC; 18, map of the trade empire, from Jackson W. Moore, Jr., BENT'S OLD FORT: AN ARCHEOLOGICAL STUDY (Boulder and Denver: Pruett Publishing Company and the State Historical Society of Colorado, 1973), p. 2 (NPS); 21, 23, 26 (portrait of Ceran St. Vrain by C. Waldo Love), SHSC; 28 and 29, artwork by Karen Williamson (SHSC); 30, A.E. Reynolds, "Family Papers"; 31, HARPER'S NEW MONTHLY MAGAZINE 35 (July 1867):145 (SHSC); 32, courtesy Denver Public Library Western History Department (DPLW); 34, SHSC; 35, E.G. Beckwith, REPORTS OF EXPLORATIONS FOR A ROUTE FOR THE PACIFIC RAILROAD BY CAPT. J.W. GUNNISON . . . , vol. 2 (Washington, D.C.: Government Printing Office, 1855), insert between pp. 34 and 35, in U.S., Senate, REPORTS OF EXPLORATIONS AND SURVEYS, 33d Cong., 2d sess. (SHSC); 39, courtesy Cragin Collection, Pioneers' Museum, Colorado Springs; 40, 41, 46, 47, SHSC; 49, Reynolds, "Family Papers"; 50, HARPER'S NEW MONTHLY MAGAZINE 35 (July 1867):189 (SHSC); 51, Records of the General Land Office, Cartographic Section, Washington, D.C.; 54, courtesy Bancroft Library, University of California, Berkeley; 56 and 57, artwork by Karen Williamson (SHSC); 61, NPS, "Bent's Old Fort: National Historic Site Project," May 1961, p. 7 (SHSC); 65, SHSC; 78 and 79, map, NPS, "Bent's Old Fort National Historic Site Project" (SHSC); 85, 86, Moore, BENT'S OLD FORT, pp. 15, 34, 66 (NPS); 101, NPS, BENT'S OLD FORT: MASTER PLAN, INTERPRETIVE PROSPECTUS, DEVELOPMENT CONCEPT (draft) (Washington, D.C.: Government Printing Office, 1975), p. 18 (NPS);102 and 103, artwork by Karen Williamson (SHSC); 107, original drawing of the floor plan in Grinnell Collection, Southwest Museum, Highland Park, Los Angeles, California; 108, SHSC; 109, Moore, BENT'S OLD FORT, p. 24 (NPS); 111, SHSC; 112, 113, NPS, BENT'S OLD FORT: MASTER PLAN, INTERPRETIVE PROSPECTUS, DEVELOPMENT CONCEPT, pp. 22, 23; 114, 117, 118, 119, 120, drawings by George A. Thorson, from NPS and URS/Ken R. White Company, BENT'S OLD FORT: NATIONAL HISTORIC SITE, OTERO

COUNTY, COLORADO *(1973), pp. H-1, I-9, C-1, F-6, F-7, F-3 (NPS); 121, drawing by George A. Thorson, NPS; 122, 123, NPS and URS/Ken R. White Company,* BENT'S OLD FORT, *F-9, F-4 (NPS); 123, drawing of doors by George A. Thorson, NPS; 124, NPS and URS/ Ken R. White Company,* BENT'S OLD FORT, *p. F-2 (NPS); 125, details from construction drawings, sheet A-10 (NPS); 129, 130, 131, photos courtesy Emil Gimeno, construction contractor for the fort; 132, construction drawing, sheet A-12 (NPS); 132 and 133, photo courtesy George A. Thorson; 133, 135, photos by Glenn Cuerden; 136, photo by Rosealie Merzbach, courtesy* DAILY JOURNAL *(Denver); 138 and 139, artwork by Karen Williamson (SHSC); 140, Moore,* BENT'S OLD FORT, *p. 92 (NPS); 143, "Council of Cheyennes and Delawares," by Abert, reproduced with permission from James W. Abert,* THROUGH THE COUNTRY OF THE COMANCHE INDIANS IN THE FALL OF THE YEAR 1845, *ed. John Galvin (San Francisco, Calif.: John Howell Books, 1970), facing p. 44; 144, 145, 146, 1978 photos by William L. Brown III, Harpers Ferry, NPS; 147, drawing of trade room, by Karen Williamson, Denver; 150,* BELLE VUE, NEBRASKA, TRADING POST, 1852, *by H.B. Möllhausen, reproduced with permission, from Museum für Völkerkunde, Staatliche Museen Preubischer Kulturbesitz, Berlin (West); 153, "Kota-a-to-ah, The Smoked Shield" and "Tee-toot-sah," from the* SMITHSONIAN REPORT, PART II, *1885, plate 26 and 25; 154, 155, watercolors of Sioux, by Abert, reproduced with permission from* THROUGH THE COUNTRY OF THE COMANCHE INDIANS, *entry for 8 August 1845; 158, Abert's room, photo by William L. Brown III, NPS; 158, "Scalp Dance, August 7, 1845," by Abert, reproduced with permission from* THROUGH THE COUNTRY OF THE COMANCHE INDIANS, *p. 4; 159, Merrimack Manufacturing Company trade card, courtesy American Antiquarian Society, Worcester, Massachusetts; 160, Eagle Gunpowder label, courtesy of the Eleutherian Mills Historical Library, Greenville, Delaware; 163, photo by William L. Brown III, NPS; 165, photo by Glenn Cuerden.*

Index

For convenience the following abbreviations have been used: BOF—Bent's Old Fort; BOFS—Bent's Old Fort Site; BOFS-NPS—Bent's Old Fort Site-National Park Service; DAR—Daughters of the American Revolution; NPS—National Park Service; and, SHSC—State Historical Society of Colorado. The illustrations are indicated by italicized page numbers.